PRAISE f

Gloria - married 10 years

Every woman needs to read *Wife on Purpose*. The way that Candice breaks down lofty sounding concepts and puts them into words that we understand; the way she gives real life stories and examples, makes *Wife on Purpose* so applicable and real. You'll never look at your marriage in the same way again.

Josie - married 6 years

Wife on Purpose is the book I will be marking up and using as my marriage bible for years to come. I'm not exaggerating when I say that Candice's work has changed my life and marriage. Because I've coached with her for years, I could have thought that I wouldn't get anything new from this book, but I know she always overdelivers. *Wife on Purpose* did not disappoint.

Brandi - married 22 years

I love reading anything Candice writes. It's like sitting on the sofa with an old friend and chatting over a cup of tea. Her words are simple and straightforward, tough but loving and always exactly what I need to hear. I've read her others books as well, and like them, *Wife on Purpose* offers clarity in a concise little package. This short read will give you the tools to see everything differently. Your relationships, your loved ones and especially yourself.

Cheryl - married 47 years

Witty, engaging and insightful. So cleverly written. I was captivated after the first page. *Wife on Purpose* is a very positive read.

Nikole - married 25 years

Wife on Purpose is a must read for women everywhere. I loved the insight, self-reflection and self-love this book offered me. I will definitely read this book again.

Brittanie - married 2 years
Wife on Purpose is a game changer. It helped me realize that I was just as important as my husband and I shouldn't shame myself for feeling that way.
Read this book, you won't regret it!

Jen - married 23 years
Wife on Purpose, with its descriptive analogies that are easy to see in your mind's eye, is a fun and exciting read. Pick it up to change your marriage and your life!

Brooke - married 19 years
Candice has a way of taking hard situations and presenting them as fun challenges that lead to you to discover and empower yourself. *Wife on Purpose* has so many applicable tools to help you get to work creating your ideal relationships. She brings hope, healing and self love into the process.
A must read!!

Heather - married 6 years
Wife on Purpose is a must read if you want to take control of your marriage and most importantly your relationship with you! With so many "advice columns" out there it can be easy to get dragged into the mud and be bogged down with great and helpful information...which gets you nowhere fast. Candice is able to clear a path with ease and give simple steps forward. I am excited to make more choices on purpose and create a marriage I am proud to be a part of.

Lu - married 22 years
Wife on Purpose is such a fun, easy read. Candice's examples are clear and refreshing. I feel more hopeful, more excited to dream about my marriage, our future. *Wife on Purpose* helps you realize "there is nothing wrong with you".
You can create real change!

Sara - married 17 years
I want every woman I love to read this book, whether her marriage is completely on the rocks or totally rock solid. Candice has a gift for speaking powerful truths with humor, wit, and so much love. I couldn't recommend *Wife On Purpose* more.

to my mother, Cheryl

*who is an unwavering example of never giving up
not even when crap after crap after crap keeps on piling up on your porch*

The information presented herein represents the views of the author as of the date of publication. This book is presented for informational purposes only. The author reserves the right to alter and update her opinions based on new conditions. While every attempt has been made to provide accurate information in this book, the author does not assume any responsibility for errors, inaccuracies, or omissions.

Pigurina Press

Copyright @2022 Candice Toone, MS

All rights reserved. Reprinting or reusing any or all parts of this book is permitted and encouraged, but only with the written consent of the author.

Wife on Purpose

Paperback - ISBN: 978-0-578-38096-4
eBook - ISBN: 978-0-578-38097-1

Wife on Purpose

CANDICE TOONE
MASTER CERTIFIED LIFE COACH

CONTENTS

Introduction 1

Hexagon Side 1 - Tell Yourself the Truth 11

Hexagon Side 2 - Notice your "Normal" 28

Hexagon Side 3 - Dream on Purpose 39

Hexagon Side 4 - Take Responsibility without Taking Blame 60

Hexagon Side 5 - Celebrate the 1% 78

Hexagon Side 6 - Don't Believe Everything you Think 95

How to Be a "Wife on Purpose" 110

Acknowledgements 117

About the Author 119

Be a Part of the Wife on Purpose movement 120

Happy Wife, Happy Life

"Impossible is temporary." - Brooke Castillo

Introduction

Remember when you were a little girl and all the Disney princess movies taught you to believe that someday your prince would come? And then, when you were a little older, all the teen movies and rom coms led you to believe that landing the perfect guy would be the climactic pinnacle of your life story?

Me too.

And do you remember how, in the early 2000s, popular trends and social media railed against all of the above? How it was en vogue to be a "boss babe" or "shero" or "mompreneur" instead of waiting around to be swept off your feet?

Yup.

That happened.

Probably because, historically, women weren't used to being taken seriously as stand alone bastions of their own destiny. As competent creators in their own lives. Heck, up until 1974 some companies still denied women the opportunity to sign up for a credit card without first securing a male co-signer. For centuries before that, women were required to rely even more heavily on their male counterparts because women weren't allowed to vote, own property, choose their own spouse or even learn to read.

So it makes sense that many women - even now, in modern times - sensitively attune their efforts toward keeping the men around them happy. For hundreds of thousands of years, male approval was literally the deciding factor between a woman's life and death, between her safety and slavery. No wonder so many of us gals are still pretty concerned with whether or not our husband is pleased. It's in our history, our very genes, to believe that a man's disapproval could have catastrophic results for us. Because, in the not so distant past, that was often the truth.

Besides, your grandmothers and aunties probably told you

something similar at your bridal or baby showers. They meant well. They thought their advice would protect you, and it might have in their day. To be fair, some of their suggestions around how to care for your man might still be useful to you now. And a lot of it might be outdated and unnecessary.

Please hear me say that I'm not holding any sort of grudge against men.

Really.

I'm not.

I know that most men are good guys trying to do right by their loved ones while shouldering an immense amount of their own unique flavor of pressure. They are tasked with lots of tough jobs that they aren't always well-equipped to do: single-handedly support a family, grow big biceps, be chivalrous without being a chauvinist and never cry about any of it for any reason, ever. I'm sure that living under all of those "rules" is a pretty big drag for our guys, and I genuinely believe that most men are doing their absolute best in response to impossible standards.

Still, it's pretty clear that their best really, really sucks sometimes.

Consider how that truth might not be the end of the world.

Maybe we can allow space for things to suck without accepting that they'll stay that way.

Because our best - yours and mine - really, really sucks at times too.

And still, we all try.

So let's take a collective breath and get on with the story.

Here's what I know: true happiness lies in figuring out how to care for yourself well while also allowing others (specifically husband) to offer you support, protection and nurturance. This can be challenging when that support, protection and nurturance look a little bit different than what you might have expected. It's actually a skill to

Introduction

receive those gestures, especially when you're looking for one version and he hands you another. And it's an advanced - I might even say impossible - skill to receive from your husband when you aren't already in the habit of giving that support, protection and nurturance to yourself.

Developing those skills is what *Wife on Purpose* is all about.

As I'm sure you've noticed, romance stories often involve a lot of waiting and wishing and wondering and pining until, finally, the couple connects with a kiss in the rain or a ride off into the sunset.

But what if you didn't have to wait for anything?

Like, ever.

Unless, for some reason, you *wanted* to.

My guess is, those happy-looking, in-love ladies from the silver screen actually did a lot of behind the scenes work that didn't make the final film cut because, well, the hard work part of a relationship just isn't all that entertaining.

I get it.

Still, regardless of what movie producers might say, entertainment value is not the same thing as actual value. My work as a Master Certified Life Coach (and a Marriage and Family Therapist before that) continually shows me how the internal work each woman does to reconnect with herself - her desires, her strengths and her boundaries - is the most valuable part of the story.

It's not flashy.

It's not always fun.

But it IS what fuels her to create the marriage she's always wanted.

It's also what helps her purposefully decide to sit back sometimes and stop hustling so hard to get the things in life that *are* worth the wait (more on that in *Wife on Pause*, the companion book to *Wife on Purpose*).

Right now, I challenge you to pause your reading and take a closer look at the guy you married. For the next 10 minutes, allow yourself to see everything - the fabulous and the flaws, the attractive and the awful. Open your brain to consider the reasons behind his quirks and his bad habits. Make room to celebrate his qualities. Review your happiest memories and recall your darkest times.

Write it all down if that helps you.

Don't worry, you don't have to show it to anyone.

You can even burn the paper later if you want to.

Breathe deep.

Roll your shoulders back and wiggle your hands.

Then write, write, write.

You done? Great.

Now set the paper aside until tomorrow.

When you read it all again in the morning, take care to check in with your gut feeling and the pulse of your heart. Combine the words you wrote with the input from your body. Roll it all around to help you access your own wisdom and your unique intuition. From there, you can decide **on purpose** if the relationship you have with your husband is worth doing the work we're about to embark on together.

Yes?

No?

Either answer is okay.

Truly.

Remember that you staying or going is not a question of "who deserves what" or "who should put up with whom and why". None of that decision can be based on what your husband is willing to hand you. Instead, place the focus on what you are willing to consciously and purposely pick up and take into your life. Might sound like: *"I really love this guy **and** I'm willing to stay with him even though I will never understand that thing he does."* or maybe *"I'm all in on this*

Introduction

relationship **and** *that doesn't mean I have to agree with his view on that."* Could also sound like, *"I love him* **and** *I'm not willing to include the consequences of his decisions in my life anymore."* or possibly *"I don't love him anymore* **and** *that doesn't mean I have to stop loving me."*

Whatever you decide, do your best to make sure your choice is based on telling yourself the whole truth. Because the more often you tell yourself the whole truth about ***everything***, the more trust you'll build with yourself. Self-trust is the foundation for purposeful living, so let's all make the commitment to purposefully cultivate more self-trust in everything we do.

We'll learn more about "The How" as we go.

For now it's enough to know that self-trust is a big part of the goal.

To start, consider your option to be super deliberate about the guy you are with and the kind of relationship you are in - because whether or not it seems so, both things are 100% your choice. Your relationship with your husband is continuously colored by the stories you tell about him and the things you choose to believe. Honestly examining your stories and beliefs becomes a whole lot easier when you are committed to having a solid relationship with yourself. That means you've gotta let yourself know what you know without making yourself wrong for knowing it. Don't try to pretend something isn't true just because it isn't flattering. You've also gotta call yourself out (in the most loving way possible) for where you might be exaggerating the issues and/or passively accepting something you'd really rather not allow.

Generate enough safety and love for yourself *from* yourself that you can honestly acknowledge the times when you are holding yourself hostage to the choices you are making without holding yourself accountable for your role in creating the situation. I know it might sound crazy right now, but claiming responsibility for something you don't like can actually be quite empowering. If you are the one creating the issue, then YOU are the one who can uncreate it without having to wait for anyone else to do anything differently. That's freedom.

Uncreating a situation you don't like will require that you don't judge yourself for the times you allowed him to cross your boundaries or ignore your needs. You probably had a very good reason for doing so at the time. It was probably some version of keeping the peace and going along to get along. You didn't want to rock the boat or upset your in-laws. You thought you were protecting your kids or your financial resources. You wanted the vacation to proceed smoothly, so you let some things slide. Why not decide right now that all of your reasons were good reasons and were valid at the time?

Then, if you find that some of the choices you made in the past aren't turning out so hot in the present, it's important to remember that choices are never a one and done. Whether or not you see it now, it's true that you are making a new choice in every moment.

All day every day.

That's freedom again.

When you find yourself wanting a different sort of relationship, it's your opportunity to purposefully notice when you're blaming him for your woes without also figuring out how you can more clearly advocate for what you want. You don't have to keep bending and shifting and accommodating. You don't have to go without. You can make requests of him. When you choose to believe you are worth getting what you want, you can more easily set the expectation that the two of you will work together to figure it out. However long it takes. And not because you are sticking it to him or taking away from what he wants in life. You'll work together on purpose because you believe in your ability to be a partnership. Even if you are very bad at

Introduction

that right now. You know that what's good for you is also good for him. Even if he doesn't see it yet. Even if one (or both) of you whine a little bit (or a lot) along the way.

Remember, even though you probably think you are, you are almost never making a choice between conflict *or* no conflict. The real choice is between what you imagine will be external conflict with him *or* internal conflict when you abandon yourself.

I know it might seem like it's easier to manage your own internal conflict. It's possible that, whether you realize it or not, you've gotten pretty good at doing the mental gymnastics required to make things work when you don't really want to. Or maybe you're just excellent at stuffing your feelings.

Been there.

And what I know is that ignored internal conflicts don't lay down and go to sleep. They fester. They poison. They erupt - and when they do, it's always so much worse than what it would have been in the beginning.

So how do you learn to care for yourself well while also allowing for husband to offer you support, protection and nurturance? Especially when his support looks a whole lot like grumbling or avoidance?

By building your own hexagon, that's how.

Have you seen "Bee Movie"? Circa 2007?

I only caught the opening scene - on a TV mounted in the ceiling while my six-year-old got his teeth cleaned - but let me tell you, it was money. The voiceover dialogue as we watched the Bees in the movie wake up to their world opened my mind to an unexpected way of thinking about marriage. Allow me to recap:

"According to all know laws of aviation, there is no way that a bee should be able to fly. Its wings are too small to get its fat little body off the groun. The bee, of course, flies anyway. Because bees don't care what humans think is

impossible."

What might be different in your marriage if you didn't care about what humans think is impossible? If you knew that your husband's mood doesn't have to dictate your day? If you believed your worth was non-negotiable - even when he implies otherwise? If you understood that it's possible to love him unconditionally while completely disagreeing with his behavior?

You can have the freedom that comes with those beliefs, Bee.

The shift is easier than you think.

Keep on reading and I'll show you how.

Honeybees have evolved over time to skillfully build hexagonal honeycomb cells. When bees make hexagons in their hives, the six-sided shapes fit together perfectly to make very efficient use of the space whilst using as little wax as possible to keep it all togehter.

How would that be?

To make highly-evolved use of the space in your head and your heart while efficiently conserving resources AND keeping it all together.

I say we do it. Using the following six sides to our metaphorical hexagons:

Hexagon Side 1 - Tell Yourself the Truth
Hexagon Side 2 - Notice your "Normal"
Hexagon Side 3 - Dream on Purpose
Hexagon Side 4 - Take Responsibility without Taking Blame
Hexagon Side 5 - Celebrate the 1%
Hexagon Side 6 - Don't Believe Everything you Think

When you start approaching your marriage with your personal hexagon in place, you'll easily see your unique path toward more happiness and connection in your marriage. Though the specifics will be vary based on your huband and your marriage, it's likely that your

Introduction

path will play out in one of two ways: either you'll challenge who you believe your current guy to be and discover he's a lot better than you thought he was OR you'll see it's time to make a new choice and find a new guy. Either realization will be a gift.

Relationships stretch us - by design. So whether you stay or go, consider the truth that there will always be problems to solve and misunderstandings to mop up. This book won't change that for you - nothing can.

Our work here will simply help you be more purposeful in the marriage you're creating. It's my promise to you that by the end of this book, you'll have everything you need to make a decision about whether to change the story you've been telling about your marriage or change your choice about who you'll spend forever with.

It's all up to you.

Tell the Truth

"The truth may set you free, but first it will piss you off." - Gloria Steinem

Hexagon Side One

Hexagon Side One

FULL DISCLOSURE: If I hadn't chosen life coaching as my career, I likely would have bailed on the process of examining my mind long ago. This stuff ain't easy. It's tough coming face to face with yourself and all you've created. Rooting out the limiting beliefs that lead you to feel hopelessly trapped can be icky, stinky work. The rewards are surely worth it, but the ride can be pretty rough.

When I first started digging around in my brain, I doubted that these methods would work to heal wounded marriages. No way you could convince me that one person working - tirelessly and all on her own - could change the tone of an entire relationship.

Admittedly, it does take a great deal of trust in God, The Universe and Mother Earth (or whatever it is you believe in) to open your vulnerabilities and loosen your grip on the story you've been telling for most of your marriage. It's a bit unnerving to consider that something new could be true.

You probably started up this self-help type of study because you were hurting or dissatisfied in some way. Know that it's common for some flavor of fear to pop up as women embark on a purposeful exploration of their marriages. Usually sounds like: *What if it's like this forever? What if I end up alone? Maybe we've screwed things up beyond any hope of repair...*

Don't you feel scared just reading those sentences?

Imagine *thinking* them - all day long.

Maybe you already are thinking thoughts like those all day long.

Yikes.

And here's the rub: when you feel scared, it's natural to crave everything working in a predictable, familiar way that makes perfect sense to you. It's not that you are bratty or inflexible. It's more that when you already feel heightened and terrified, introducing the scary unknown on top of the uncertainty and helplessness that already exists seems like a terrible idea. It seems preferable to stick with what you've always believed - even when what you've always believed looks nothing like what you want the truth to be. Even when what you've always believed is incredibly painful.

Scared people, as a general rule, aren't great at trust. Not in their loved ones. Not in the process. Not in themselves.

Especially not in themselves.

Most of the wives I work with are pretty used to sacrificing themselves in order to care for someone else. Women are taught to believe that our value comes in what we can offer to others, so making ourselves available around the clock seems like what we're "supposed to do." Under the mantle of family nurturer, women often require themselves to bend and twist and stretch and give - often close to the point of breaking. They attend to themselves as an afterthought if they attend to themselves at all. For many of us, all of that just seems normal. Plus, society rewards women for caring in this way. We call them "righteous" and "charitable" and "noble" when they do. And it's not all bad. There are definitely some perks that go along with selfless service.

But... moderation in all things, amirite?

When your only focus is the well-being of others, your self-trust erodes without you even noticing. If you expect yourself to smile and make the best of it while your soul is dissolving, your inner self learns that you're more likely than not to ignore her needs.

Ignored needs breed resentment.

Resentment destroys relationships.

Especially since we sometimes expect our husbands to notice our needs and carve out resources to meet them. Husbands are almost always pretty bad at that. Why? Because they are also terrible mind readers. And even though it seems like it should be, mind reading is not a skill that improves with time or proximity. So whether you've been married 5 years or 67 years, my guess is you'll still have to tell your husband directly if you want or need something in particular.

I'll pause while your brain tells you what a bummer that is.

Maybe so.

But it could also be a huge relief (for both of you) to clearly communicate about what's going to keep your marriage happily humming along.

So let's talk about telling the truth.

To you.

To him.

Even when it's hard.

I'm pretty confident that you are already very good at telling the truth. My guess is that you are not likely to purposefully deceive anyone in your life. I also know that many of us fall victim to "Christmas sweater mentality". We smile and pretend that we like something - even when we don't - because we really don't want the other person to feel bad. Challenge is, when you force yourself to do what you think is protecting other people's feelings, you're no longer paying attention to your own.

Telling the whole truth, from a place of love, opens up room for everyone's feelings to matter. Including yours.

So how can we tell the truth and consider all the feelings involved? Glad you asked. I imagine you've heard Carl Douglas' song, "Kung Fu Fighting". If not, you're welcome to put this book down for a bit and find it on YouTube.

I'm happy to wait.

When you listen, you'll hear the line: "Everybody was Kung Fu fighting". For decades, most people accepted that lyric as a plausible truth. No one really bothered to check the validity of this claim. We all just went with Douglas' assertion and danced along.

Tell the Truth

Years after I first heard the song, I saw a T-shirt printed with the graphic: "Surely not everyone was Kung Fu fighting" across the front. When I read the shirt, I laughed right out loud. And I bought it immediately.

This is the essence of telling yourself the truth.

Start by noticing, on purpose, when something is generally accepted as true and then poke around in that line of thinking to see whether it serves you or not to go on believing it. For example:

Caring husbands remember the details of their wife's week.

Bills should be paid as soon as they are received.

Good grades are better.

My parents should be welcomed into our home during the holidays.

It all sounds lovely. Like a beautiful picture of the way the best marriages go. But it's all poison. Because when your husband forgets about your doctor appointment or complains about how long your mother is staying at Thanksgiving, it feels like something has gone wrong. Like your marriage is less connected or less successful in some way. Because none of it is going the way it was "supposed to".

So painful to look at the life you've built with the man you chose that way.

Without conscious supervision, all of our brains cook up wonderful sounding expectations. And when those expectations aren't met...

Tragedy.

Disappointment.

Hurt.

Doubt.

Fortunately, there's another way. Telling yourself the whole truth makes it possible for you to get a leg up on the unconscious programming that was bred into your brain as you watched movies, read books, listened to songs and paid attention to the relationships around you. Becoming conscious of your previously unquestioned expectations helps you decide if you really want to keep the rules you have for him, for yourself and for your marriage.

You don't have to make those decisions from a place of dejected resignation. You can do it from a place of purposeful curiosity and genuine fascination for the complex husband you've chosen to accompany you on this adventure we call married life.

This is usually the part where women say something like: "So… what? I'm just supposed to have NO expectations of him at all? He can just do whatever and that's it?!"

I get why women ask that.

And no, that's not what I'm saying.

I actually think the healthiest thing you can do for your marriage is to get super, extra, ultra, crystal clear about your expectations and your preferences for how you want everything to go. When you really know what your preferences and expectations are, it is one million times easier to tell the truth about them.

Then, remind yourself that all of your preferences and expectations are just optional beliefs that you've adopted.

Like lyrics you've heard over and over.

Surely not EVERYONE was Kung Fu fighting.

Some people - probably even a LOT of people - definitely were.

But others weren't. Some people were plugging their ears. Others were doing yoga or sleeping. Still others were back in the kitchen making cookies, completely oblivious to the whole dance fight party thing going on in the streets.

There are LOTS of approaches to married life.

The key is to find and live from the ones that get you the marriage you want to have.

All of that rests on a commitment to telling the truth.

To you.

Tell the Truth

To him.

Let's start with telling yourself the whole truth first. I'll offer some scenarios and then we'll practice identifying the whole truth without making any of it wrong. Ready? Go!

Scenario 1: Brand new neighbor comes over unannounced to let you and your husband know that the fence line (which was built prior to either of you moving into this neighborhood) actually doesn't follow the property line. Neighbor says that some of his land is in your yard and he wants you to buy the land back from him. After the neighbor leaves, husband says he's considering paying the $10k the neighbor asked for.

Painful story: *Husbands should protect our resources above all else and my husband isn't. Why does he always choose everyone else over me?*

The Whole Truth: *I'm afraid because I'm believing that my husband is choosing someone else over me. It hurts when I believe that might be true, but it could be. It's also possible that he thinks he IS protecting our resources by trying to keep the peace with our neighbors. I don't have to agree with him and I can still love him. There is probably more to his thought process that I don't yet know. I can also state my opinion that I don't think we should pay and give myself space to explain why.*

Notice how we don't have to make fear wrong here. We also don't have to agree with husband's belief that maybe the neighbor should be paid for the land. We can acknowledge that husband considering the neighbor's request might mean that he doesn't care about you, but also consider how it might not mean that at all.

Scenario 2: Your sister and her family are headed to the beach during a scheduled school break. You and your husband didn't plan to do anything special and actually didn't realize the break was even coming up. Exactly like what happened during the last school break.

Painful story: *We are never going to be the kind of family who plans vacations ahead of time. We'll always just throw something dumb together at the last minute or stay home. We are wasting this time we have while all of us are still living all together. They'll never have any fun memories of growing up.*

The Whole Truth: *Neither of us planned ahead for the school break. I didn't confirm the dates and it's likely he was waiting on me to do so. It's even possible that he didn't think about it at all. Also, both of us care about making good memories with our kids. I am upset because I held myself back when I thought he'd complain or make the planning hard. I might be right about his habit of doing that. I also used that possibility as a reason to not plan. It's okay that I did that and I don't have to keep doing it if I don't want to.*

Notice how we don't have to pretend that we don't want husband to help out with the planning or at least make it go easier. We also don't have to talk ourselves into believing it's okay to just stay home if that's really not what we want. When we tell the whole truth it's so much easier to notice opportunities to shift this pattern moving forward - if we decide that we want something different to happen next time.

Scenario 3: Husband asks you where you want to go for dinner. You say you don't care and ask him to choose. Husband perceives your facial expression to tell a different story. He huffs, throws his hands in the air and asks why you have to be so difficult all the time.

Painful story: *Wow. That's ridiculous. We can't even discuss dinner. How are we ever going to be able to discuss anything important? He's just going to pick what he wants anyway - or complain - so there's no point in me choosing.*

The Whole Truth: *I don't believe he will take my opinion into account and I am holding back from sharing because of that belief. I am also pissed because I want my opinion to matter. I also think I'm not allowed to be pissed because he won't care how I feel and that makes me even more pissed. He's also not wrong that I'm being difficult. I kind of am and it makes sense why I would be if I believe my voice doesn't count. I can also see how my keeping quiet doesn't really help us connect. And I'm still afraid to say what I want.*

Notice how including the whole truth introduces some compassion into the interaction. Compassion feels more open than contempt, so it can be useful to everyone to figure out how to get there - especially when we remember that compassion doesn't have to mean we give in if we don't want to.

Filling your brain with the whole truth will do a lot to help you see how many options you really have. From there, you can make purposeful choices that align with the kind of woman and wife that you really want to be, which is a terrific place to start.

But what about him? How do you go about telling the truth, the WHOLE truth, to him? Well.. what if we just did the exact same thing? I'll offer some scenarios and then we'll practice how you might say the whole truth when you are talking to him out loud - without making either of you wrong as you sort things out together.

Scenario 1: You and husband went to bed angry last night after an argument. When you wake up, the first thing out of his mouth is a string of insults and accusations.

Painful story: *He thinks he can talk to me however he wants to and there's no way for me to stop it. I'm stuck and he's mean. I really hate him sometimes.*

The Whole Truth sounds like this out loud: *"I get that you're mad. I hear that. I want to hear your point because I love you and I care about us. I'm also not willing to hear your point in this way, so I'm going to go take a shower and get ready for my day. I would appreciate you giving me space in the bathroom. I'll be out in 30 mins and we can try again then."*

Note: it's important to make sure everything you are saying is actually true. If you don't want to hear him out or you're not able to access love for him in that moment, don't say those things. Simply omit that line and go straight to being honest about what you are and are not willing to be available for. That might sound more like this:

"I get that you're mad. I hear you. I'm too mad to listen to you right now and I need some more time. Doesn't mean I won't ever listen. I just don't think now is a good time. I'm going to go take a shower and get ready for my day. I would appreciate you giving me space in the bathroom. I'll be out in 30 mins and I'll check in to see if I feel more ready to hear you then. I know that might be hard for you to hear. I'm sure you don't want to wait and I understand that. I'm not trying to be difficult - I just need a little more time."

Pro tip: expect that when you start telling your husband the whole truth, he might not love it. That's okay. This is a different strategy than how you two have interacted before, so of course he might be thrown off.

He'll regain his balance.

I promise.

Your only job is to focus on the truth and support yourself in telling it as kindly as you can. This takes practice and you'll probably screw it up sometimes. Not a problem. This is a new skill you are learning and you're learning it because you want to create more connection with your sweetheart.

Honesty will do that.

Every time.

And it may take a little getting used to - for both of you.

Hang in there.

Scenario 2: Husband is sitting on the couch watching TV while you are doing chores and tidying up after breakfast on Saturday.

Painful story: *How is it possible that he doesn't see how much needs to be done around here? I have to do everything. All alone. Every time. Who does he think he is to take a break when I never get one?*

The Whole Truth sounds like this out loud: *"Hey babe. I know you work really hard and it's great that you're getting to take a break. You deserve some rest on the weekend. We also have x, y and z to get done today. Which of those would you like to take on and when? I'd like us to work together so I can have some rest too. How can we make that happen?"*

Again, take care that you only say what's actually true. If you don't think he works hard or you're not sure he deserves some rest, adjust that part to match what's true for you. Note that you don't have to absolve him from helping. You also don't have to figure out a way to smile and do it all yourself - or you can if you want to.

Great news is: it's always your call.

When you support yourself in believing that your desires are valid, it's a lot easier to ask for what you want. And if, for example, you don't yet believe that you have the right to advocate for the sharing of household duties, it's probably time to back up to the step where you get curious and tell *yourself* the truth about why not. Maybe you'll find a reason you like and then drop your desire for his help or maybe you'll figure out that you don't like your reasons for requiring yourself to do it all on your own. That answer will probably be different for each woman, which is the magical thing about telling yourself the whole truth. You find out what *you* want to believe on purpose and you build your marriage from there.

Scenario 3: You and husband randomly run into your kid's handsome baseball coach when you're out for a walk one evening. After you make introductions and chat for a bit, you and husband keep on walking. Several paces later, husband turns to you and says, "Well, well, well... you were certainly excited to see *him*!"

Painful story: *He doesn't trust me. I'm so tired of him pushing his insecurities on me. Why can't he just believe me when I say that I'm not out looking? He must think I don't have any standards or loyalties at all. Or... maybe **he's** out looking so he assumes that I would be too... this sucks.*

The Whole Truth sounds like this out loud: *"You're right. I was happy to see him. Glad that you two got the chance to meet. He does a really good*

Tell the Truth

job coaching and I want to support him because he supports our kid. It also sounds like you think I'm interested in him which I'm not. It makes me sad to think you might not trust me and my commitment to us. What's that about? Can I help?"

It would be pretty easy to make his comment mean something bad about you ("He thinks I'm disloyal"), bad about him ("He's so controlling and paranoid."), or bad about your marriage ("There's no trust here."), but all of those things feel terrible. Happy thing is: It's also an option to interpret his comment as a bid for more connection with his one and only (you) and then get curious about how you can reassure and flirt with him a little if that's what you are willing to give.

Might sound like this: *"I mean, I guess he's handsome and all, but I barely noticed because I've got you looking sexy in that T-shirt right here next to me."*

bats eyelashes

Both scenarios are available to you. Which one sounds like more fun?

You can pick fun whenever you want to.

And you never have to.

Your call.

I know you've heard that a working marriage is just that - work. But what kind of work?

THIS kind of work.

The kind where you allow the whole truth to be true. The kind where you tell the whole truth as often and as kindly as you can. The kind where you understand that telling the whole truth will sometimes be very painful and disorienting in the short run. The kind where you open up to the idea that sometimes the "short" run might last for a long while. The kind where you know that you'll stay with yourself, comfort yourself and support yourself until you create the kind of relationship you really want to live in.

Most wives try to improve their marriage by looking for ways to bend and adapt and accommodate their husbands.

And sure, most marriages will include some of that.

What's also true is that those mental acrobatics and emotional gymnastics are WAY LESS NECESSARY than you think. Telling the truth as often as you can, without apology or justification, is the key to helping you see how you actually don't need to twist yourself in knots in order for your marriage to survive. In fact, the opposite is true. When you open yourself up and purposefully choose to impact your space, that's when your marriage will gain the breath and connection required to thrive.

Sometimes women tell me that they can't tell the truth because if they do, everything will crumble. Maybe. But what if we all tried on a little more faith than that? What if you imagined a world where husband could shoulder the things you want to say? And where you are fully capable of supporting yourself in saying them?

You could decide that none of the current disconnection between you is dangerous because all of it is really just a fascinating puzzle to put back together. You could choose to live from the foregone conclusion that you two are, for sure, going to live a long and (mostly) happy life together. It's an option to let those beliefs give you the freedom to see how your only job is figuring out the daily details of how you're going to create the life you want as a united team.

That's work worth doing.

Of course there will be moments, days or even years where the connection seems less stable. It's likely there will be tense times when you're not sure you're gonna make it. And in those times, the whole truth will save the day again. Sounds like: *"This is the part where everything sucks. I'm not sure how this is going to turn out. I also know that every good story has some conflict. Maybe that's all that's happening here. Good thing I'm such a bad ass protagonist. I'm sure I'll figure out how to take care of me. And us. I'm not in a hurry. I can totally handle this."*

What might be different about your current problems if you believed all of the above were true? Could be kinda fun to think about.

Before we wrap up our discussion of this pillar, I've got an important caveat to share. I invite you to read through it twice. This part matters that much.

Paying attention to your thinking and choosing your thoughts on purpose does not mean that you are trying to figure out how to twist your perspective enough to ignore "bad signs" or "red flags". You never, ever, ever, ever have to accept anything that you don't want to accept.

Ever.

It's also a gift you give yourself to be objective and purposeful about what you decide to label as a "bad sign" or "red flag". Tell yourself the truth about why you're labeling the behavior or attribute that way and make sure you like your reason. Know that your reasons for liking or not liking something don't have to make sense to anyone else. Your only job is to know what you know and support yourself in knowing it.

Let's take an example.

Say your husband curses at you when you fight. Many people would label that behavior to be a "red flag". It's totally possible that calling cursing a "red flag" is the exact right thing to do. If you don't like it, you don't have to stick around when it's happening. Ever.

Period.

End of story.

There's nothing wrong with you if you don't want to roll with it when you're being cursed at. Doesn't mean you're over sensitive or that you lack compassion or that you're not taking responsibility for your part in the conflict.

He might try to tell you so, but he'd be confused.

You don't have to let his confusion confuse you.

It's absolutely possible to show him compassion and take responsibility for your role in the fight while still saying a hard "no" to being cursed at.

Really. It is.

Other thoughts are also available to you about his decision to curse. You could think: *"Wow. He's really upset and he's not sure how to handle his emotions well. Good thing I am willing to de-escalate this."* You could think: *"Lots of people swear when they are riled up. This means nothing about me. And I don't have to respond right now. He can try again when he's gotten a hold of himself - and I love him anyway."* Or maybe it's more like: *"I'm going to ignore those words and try to decipher his underlying message because cursing isn't really that big of a deal in my mind. If he starts calling me names though… then I'm out."*

There are infinite other ways to tell the story.

None are "correct" or "morally superior".

Thought work simply shows you how you create your experience. It's not meant to imply that you "should" create THIS experience or THAT one. There's no right way to do marriage - expect the one YOU decide is right.

The only reason to pay attention to the story you are telling is to help yourself see if the story you are telling is getting YOU more or less of the experience you want to have. It's always your option to steer your brain toward the story that helps you feel the way you want to feel - whatever that is.

Which 100% does **NOT** mean that you should seek to feel amazing about everything.

That would make NO sense at all.

The point is to remember that you feel the way you feel because of the story you are telling and if you ever decide you want to have a different emotional experience, you hold all of the cards to make that happen. Whew.

You never have to change how you feel.

You won't win a medal for "most caring wife" or "most evolved human" if you do.

The point is to tell yourself the whole truth about why you feel the way you do AND to tell yourself the whole truth about whether or not you want to keep that feeling going.

Sometimes you'll be too tired to reframe your thinking.

Other times you simply won't want to.

It's all part of the human experience.

The more often you tell yourself the truth that humans aren't meant to feel amazing all of the time, the less distressed you'll be about the crappy moments of your marriage. When you aren't distressed about the crappiness, you're more likely to get curious about what you're creating. When you tell yourself the truth about how you're creating all of it - *without making yourself wrong for creating any of it* - that's when you'll claim your power and calm your fears.

When you're honest with yourself about everything going on in your brain, you'll be more able to do the hard work of connecting to yourself right now, today. When you're solidly connected to yourself in everything you think and feel, it'll be so much easier to connect with him over the long term.

Everybody wins.

Nice work, you.

Notice your "Normal"

*"I don't know who discovered water,
but I'm pretty sure it wasn't a fish." - Marshall McLuhan*

Hexagon Side Two

Notice your "Normal"

If you've ever seen an episode of a sitcom centered around a married couple, you know that stereotypes around the husband-wife dyad are alive and well:

- Having a husband is like having another irresponsible, sloppy child.
- He's only after one thing and you're gonna have to give it on his birthday.
- You're gonna decorate and he's gonna hate your throw pillows.
- He's an idiot who will need a giant list of instructions when you leave town.
- Wanting to do anything on your own, without your spouse, is a sign of trouble.

Reading through all of that all at once makes it easy to see how those claims are kinda silly and pretty oversimplified. Maybe so. And… there are likely some shenanigans of a similar sort coloring your marriage.

Mine too.

What?!

Yep.

Every married person has unconsciously adopted some "rules" around the way things work in their marriage. You can find your unique flavor of this by listening for the following phrases as they rattle around in your brain or roll off your tongue:

"Oh. I know he'd never…"

"That's just the way we do things."

"It's like that every year."

"I can't even imagine what it would be like if he didn't…"

"That's something I'm used to handling."

I know it might seem like your marriage is set up the way it is because he's just so stubborn or oblivious or apathetic. I would not be surprised to hear you say you believe there's no point in trying to make a change. You might be right. Just consider that possibly... just maybe... **you decided** to believe that there is no point in trying to make a change, and that's why things aren't changing. And maybe... just maybe... that "no point" thing isn't actually true.

He said something or didn't do something.

You decided, for whatever reason, that it wasn't worth it to advocate for something else.

So you went along.

And now here you are.

That's the whole truth.

It's not good. It's not bad. It just is. And once you see it, you can decide if you want to keep it going the way that it's been going up to this point or not.

Now, I can almost hear you telling me that you really, really can't make him change. You would if you could and you've certainly tried. And yes, I agree. You can't change him. He's never going to do anything unless he wants to do it. That's true for him and it's true for you.

You don't ever do anything unless you want to do it either.

Even when it doesn't seem like you have a choice, I promise you do. Unless you're in some sort of extreme hostage situation, which I'm guessing you aren't since you're reading this book. So, let's pause for a second with pure fascination around how the brain loves to run away to outlier examples, like hostages. When that happens, get curious about why a part of you thinks disproving a concept that could be helpful is the best way to spend your energy. What's making you fight so hard to keep your pain? Especially when the option of reclaiming your freedom to choose is also available?

Telling yourself the whole truth about why your life is set up the

Notice your "Normal"

way it is gives you the gift of seeing the "normal" you've accepted. Once you see it, you can then decide if you want to keep it or change it. You can start paying attention to that decision and make it on purpose, over and over, in lots of little aspects of your life. When you do, the "normal" you are living will inch closer and closer to matching your preferences for the future.

So fun.

We've discussed how unmet needs breed resentment. We've talked about how many of us believe that our unmet needs are our husband's fault. And how that might not be true. Instead, what could be happening is that you agreed to let your needs go unmet at lots of tiny points along the way. You did that for good reasons. Reasons that might not be working out anymore. Reasons that made up the "normal" you've come to accept.

I know you might be thinking something like: *"but we share in the decision making..."* or *"he makes all the money, so what am I supposed to do...?"* or *"he has really particular ideas that he's made SUPER clear, so that's the end of the conversation - it's not worth fighting over."*

Yes.

To all of that.

And now what?

Do you know what rules you've accepted about what happens if you don't see eye to eye on something? Are you aware of how the default decision making tends to go? Are you good with that strategy? Or not? What attitudes make up your "normal" about money? If he's making most of it or even all of it, what then? What if you are the one bringing home the bulk of the income? And if he states his preference super clearly, maybe repeatedly, what does that mean for the two of you? What's your "normal" when difficult conversations are at play?

It will always be true that you can't make him change. It's also likely that all of us have more choices available to us than "make him change" or "accept what is." If your "normal" didn't include limiting yourself to those extreme options, what then?

You can certainly accept whatever it is as many times as you want if accepting your "normal" is really and truly what you want to do. Sometimes the thing is actually not worth the effort required to challenge it. If that's the case for you, I hear you. Go ahead and settle into your "normal" and get on with your night. Just do it because you want to, not because you believe it's your only option.

If you find that you really don't want to accept your current "normal" anymore, consider what it might be like for you to believe you can influence what "normal" means in your marriage. We sometimes take, as a given, that women have less power in the relationship. It makes sense if that's what you believe to be the case for the two of you. That's how most of us have seen things arranged for centuries. Through nobody's fault or ill-intent, we probably learned that "he's in charge" dynamic from our parents who learned it from theirs and so on.

Challenge is, when you believe you have less power in your relationship, you're more likely to negotiate with yourself about what you "can" and "can't" bring up for re-evaluation. You'll hem and haw about where you "should" and "shouldn't" shine a possibly painful light. When you censor yourself in this way, you reinforce a power differential that you don't really want. One that he may not want either. One that he might not even be aware of because it doesn't tend to play out in the backdrop of his self-talk.

Through these types of internal negotiation, women teach themselves to ask for less. We worry that we'll get in trouble, so we stifle our self-advocacy efforts. We don't want to "pay for it later" so we give up and make it work - even when we'd rather not. Not surprisingly, the giving up leads to a whole bunch of nothing

Notice your "Normal"

changing while we silently seethe or ignore ourselves completely. Or maybe it's more like we get worked up and bitter, which ends in heated, blame-filled conversations that go nowhere quick.

It's our option to see those flavors of "normal" playing out and to then decide on purpose if we are willing to be wrong about the way we think our marriage has to work. Maybe it's "worked" that way to this point - you're still together after all - but what if it doesn't have to keep working that way?

What if staying together is just a VERY low bar for relationship success?

What if you could create something more? Something closer to what you imagined you'd have when you said, "I do."?

Creating something more requires your willingness to be wrong about what you believe he'll listen to and wrong about what you believe you can require. I know that admitting you were wrong can seem like a scary and painful venture, but what if it doesn't have to be? What if being wrong in this sense is like learning you were wrong about your airplane seat assignment? You thought your spot was in the back of the plane, middle seat, right near the lavatory. But turns out, you're supposed to be up in first class with all that extra leg room and a hot towel waiting.

Not bad, eh?

Being wrong about the stuckness in your marriage could feel the exact same way.

And advocating for a first class seat gets even easier when you remember that you could be totally fine at the back of the plane. You could make your own fun and create your own comfort even when sandwiched between two strangers, one of whom snores. Because, remember, your seatmates don't create your experience. YOU do. Whenever you want to.

Would it be harder to create the experience you want at the back of the plane?

Maybe.

Maybe not.

Right now, the back of the plane is your "normal" after all.

You can absolutely figure out how to enjoy your experience exactly where you are. My guess is that you already do enjoy your experience at least some of the time.

Learning to create love and happiness and comfort for yourself at the back of the plane more often actually makes it that much easier to advocate for moving up to first class. Why? Because when you know you can support and enjoy yourself no matter where you are sitting, it becomes a whole lot less urgent to figure out how to sit somewhere else. And when moving your seat isn't all that urgent, you'll be much more willing to take a shot at it - because the stakes are low.

You can support and cheer yourself at the back of the plane or in the front.

And you can experience peace and connection whether your husband gets through his honey-do list or not.

What if that's true?

Imagine, just for a second, that you can fully enjoy your life no matter what comes at you next. Of course, you'll like some things more than you like others - but what if none of it can shake your connection with yourself? And what if an immovable connection with yourself is all you need to create the exact marriage you really, really want?

Of course, you'll love it if you get what you are asking for.

And you'll be just fine if you don't.

When you *really* know that, your asks get bigger.

Your marriage gets better.

Your "normal" is a lot more fun.

Notice your "Normal"

I can't promise it'll be a straight, steadily climbing linear progression from where you are now to where you want to be. But I can promise that starting the climb is the surest way to get to the top.

So what are you waiting for?

I know. Your husband.

That insensitive creature of habit just won't change. There's no way.

You might be right.

But what if you aren't?

Are you willing to be wrong? Are you willing to take your marriage to first class? Even if that means you'll stumble as you climb out of your back-of-the-plane seat, bang your elbows as you move up the aisle and endure jealous glares as you make your way forward?

It's totally okay if you aren't willing to go there. You're used to your current "normal" after all. I understand if your brain is offering you the idea that you can't REALLY control things. I get it if you are still kinda thinking about hostages or people who lived through something horrific, like the Holocaust. They didn't have much of a choice, Candice, now did they?

You're right.

They didn't have much choice.

They also had some.

We can start by acknowledging again that brains love to go to extreme examples. They think that citing those stories will convince you to save your energy, which is something that brains really want to do. Also, since scared brains don't like to try out new ways of thinking (remember: unfamiliar = bad to a brain that's already worried) it makes sense if you are reluctant to try on the idea that you have more power in your marriage than you think you do.

Even if husband is stubborn and opinionated.

Even if you've never noticed your voice before.

It's also okay if you don't want to do any of this. Like I said,, you can totally get where you are going sitting in the back row of the plane. All of this is just for fun. Just if you want to. Whether you do this work or not, you are an amazing woman who retains the right to live her life exactly the way she wants to live it.

So, from here on out, if you think you might want to shake up the "normal" that's been the story of your marriage so far, I'm talking to you. Starting right now, we're going to operate from the assumption that we don't have to change husband's thoughts, comments or behaviors in order to enjoy a full and satisfying marriage. Because we are clear on the fact that satisfaction comes from the stories we choose to tell ourselves, we will consciously choose to tell satisfying stories about our marriages as often as possible.

AND

We will figure out how to pull for the changes we'd like to see.

It doesn't have to be one or the other.

When you really, really know that's true - that you can tell a satisfying story and still want more or different - you'll be unstoppable.

When you are willing to purposefully notice your "normal", you give yourself the gift of seeing whether or not you are narrating your marriage in a way that will enable you to create the relationship you really, really want. That awareness is your very most precious superpower, and it's all you need to change your entire marriage if you are willing to use your power when it's hardest for you to see.

Commit to notice when you are embarking on a journey you expect has a dismal conclusion. Know that it's always your option to choose another path. You can do the work to figure out who you are without your painful story. If you like her life better, which I'm guessing you will, you can purposefully choose to think and act like

Notice your "Normal"

her in the daily decisions you make. As Joyce Meyer states in her book, *Healing the Soul of a Woman*, "Our true problem lies not in being wounded but in whether or not we are willing to be healed."

Healing requires you to tell yourself the truth about the "normal" you've accepted. You'll need to remind yourself that you had a good reason for accepting that normal for as long as you have AND you'll need to remind yourself that you don't have to accept it anymore if you don't want to. You can reject your "normal" from a place of love and determination. You don't have to judge or blame or burn everything down.

It can be more of a remodel than a bonfire.

So, be vigilant in recognizing when your "normal" interpretations of your marriage and your husband lead to separation and disconnection. Stay open to the idea that there could be another way to look at things. Choose that new way whenever it feels better to do so. Because when you feel better, you'll show up for yourself better and when you show up as the best version of you - that's when you'll get the fun, connected marriage you deserve.

I can't say enough that it's totally okay if you find yourself telling disempowered stories sometimes - maybe even a lot of the time, especially when you first start noticing what you'd previously tuned out because you thought it was "normal". Your "normal" stories are what you are used to, so you're likely to feel sorta comforted in telling them, even if you don't like the way they feel. The stories you tell have nothing to do with your value as a wife or your worth as a person. The only reason to pay attention to them at all is to get a new experience of your marriage if you decide that's what you want. It's simply an option - and not even a morally superior one - to open up to how you think staying in the "normal" is benefitting you and then be honest with yourself about whether it's actually working out the way you thought it would.

Contention may be the norm for your marriage right now. You can also choose to seek commonalities and connection as the "new normal" whenever you like. As long as you are paying attention and supporting yourself no matter what you see, a brand new "normal" is closer than you think.

Dream on Purpose

"The biggest adventure you can ever take is to live the life of your dreams." - Oprah Winfrey

Hexagon Side Three

What would it mean to be *truly great* in your marriage this year?

Instead of just getting through it?

Do you know?

It's okay if you don't. You wouldn't be alone in that not knowing camp.

Because of the harrowing adventures that can come from sharing your life with someone who sometimes seems like a stranger, many of us are just keeping our heads down a lot of the time.

We're trying to get through the day with as little pain as possible.

There's not always space for much more than that.

But what if there could be?

What if you expected the challenges? Welcomed them even?

I don't know a lot about professional football, but I do know that those players voluntarily go through brutal workouts and grueling trainings all season long, every year. They do it because they want to make it to the SuperBowl - the annual pinnacle of the professional football experience. They all sign up to take a beating on purpose because they believe a shot at playing in the big game makes everything else worth it.

Then they do it again, the next year and the next. Even though the vast majority of them never actually make it to the playing field on SuperBowl Sunday.

So interesting.

What if we treated our marriages a bit more like that?

I'm not saying we should sign up to be physically pummeled.

Please hear me on that.

I am floating the idea that it could be fun to have a SuperBowl-esque dream in mind for your marriage. A dream that sounds so awesome and fun and rewarding that you'd sign up - on purpose - to do the hard work and endure the heartache it takes to get there.

Even if you didn't get there as quickly as you wanted.

Even if you never got there at all.

What if you dreamed a dream so beautiful and inspiring that you'd be willing to keep working for it no matter what it took?

Let's start with just this year - the next 12 months. For just a couple minutes, allow your brain to noodle on how you really, really, really want things to be between you and your husband. Imagine a reality you'd gladly work for. Get clear on your secret dream for your marriage.

You don't have to tell me what it is.

Just ask yourself, and genuinely answer, would you rather go down trying for that secret dream or live the rest of your life with exactly what you have right now?

Essentially, would you rather lose the SuperBowl game or not play football at all?

Neither option is right or wrong. You'll simply have a different experience of your life and your relationship based on that one choice.

Be sure to make it on purpose.

My work affords me the great honor of helping women stop wondering if they married the wrong guy so they can put all that wondering energy to better use building the relationship of their dreams. Our goal is not to eliminate their problems all together, but to increase the quality of the problems they are seeking to solve.

We aren't going for NO problems.

We're going for BETTER problems.

Because human brains are problem solving machines. Your brain is always going to be scanning your environment for something to sort out, so why not give it useful, dream-building problems on purpose?

For example, you can choose to endlessly wonder why you and your husband aren't connecting like so many of your couple friends appear to be OR you could choose to figure out how to get your family on that European vacation that's been on your vision board for ages.

You can choose to keep track of how many promises he's broken OR you could figure out how to support yourself in feeling vulnerable while you open an honest discussion with him about what's been left undone.

Notice that the first two challenges - lack of connection, a sense of distrust - leave you passively spinning in pain. There's not much risk in that space. You're already feeling pretty awful. And maybe there's some comfort that comes with familiarity, some security that comes from believing you can't fall much further. Just double check with yourself that that's the type of comfort and security you want. You may "know" what to expect, but there's also very little chance of creating a new experience in that space.

The second two challenges - taking a vacation, deepening your purposeful communication - require more from you. Those options demand that you take responsibility for what you've co-created with him. They compel you to get some skin in the game and put your heart on the line.

Might sound terrifying.

I hear you.

And I know that road is the one with your dream goal at the end. It's up to you if you want to start walking towards it to claim your prize.

Many people don't dream because they don't want to be disappointed. And what's ironic is that not dreaming actually guarantees that you'll end up with less than what you really want. It may seem like not dreaming equals not hurting. But what's true is that you're simply choosing to be disappointed at the starting line. You're opting for the hurt that comes through living with unexplored possibilities instead of the hurt that might come as you get out there and pursue your dream.

So remind yourself that the choice isn't really between feeling disappointed or not feeling disappointed. The real choice is between feeling certain disappointment now or possible disappointment later. Disappointment is part of the human experience. You can choose to feel it when you lose the SuperBowl or feel it because you didn't even try out for the team. And hey - it's also possible that you'll actually win the SuperBowl and feel elated instead. Would that be worth it?

Why or why not?

Again, your answers matter less than your awareness of them. Because awareness leads to purposefulness and purposefulness is the reason you and I are having this chat. No more passive passenger role for you, Bee. You deserve way better than that. So tell yourself the truth about the "normal" you are living and decide ***on purpose*** if you'd like to dream beyond what you are used to experiencing.

You're awesome either way.

Dreaming bigger won't change how amazing you are as a human being. But it just may change your experience of your life and your relationship. Whether that's worth it is up to you.

We know that fear can cripple the cultivation of big dreams. We've also discussed how it's totally in your power to be happy and have fun in a worst case scenario - like a back row airplane seat. If you can imagine your worst case scenario and still see how you could potentially experience joy and love in that moment, it might be time to decide that there's really no reason not to go full throttle after the things you've always wanted.

Allow me to illustrate with an experience from my own life. When the COVID-19 virus hit in early 2020, my husband and I watched as the company he worked for did all kinds of creative contortions to keep employees on board. Then we watched as they cut salaries and laid off personnel. We decided together that it'd be best for him to hop off that sinking ship and start working for equity (i.e., for no pay - at least at first) at a different company.

That meant the whole of our family's expenses fell to me and my business.

Which had never been part of my plan.

Being the primary breadwinner felt like a lot of pressure. I probably wouldn't have picked that on purpose - at least not when my brand new business was just barely over a year old.

But primary breadwinner I became. (And I did pick it on purpose - even though my brain sometimes likes to tell me that Covid-19 picked it for me.)

It's been awesome and awful.

The whole time.

Like life is supposed to be.

The income itself has been amazing. I do very well in my business. My family hasn't had to adjust our lifestyle at all in the wake of my husband no longer working. So liberating to realize that I'm more than capable of providing for my family - and providing for them well. I know that many women stay in relationships they'd rather not keep because they are afraid of losing resources like housing and cash flow to care for their babies. So wild and wonderful to show myself that I can take care of us just fine - regardless of whether I choose to stay with him.

The emotional experience has been less consistently amazing. In many ways, it's fun to have him home more often. It's nice that he took over carpool and that he cooks dinner. Less fun is how husband and I don't always agree about what it means to be a "stay-at-home-parent". It's also been tough for both of us to adjust our focus to prioritize my business when both of us had always been in the habit of prioritizing his. I often felt stretched thin and resentful. Sometimes I felt left out of time with the kiddos. He felt micromanaged and judged. Sometimes he felt overwhelmed with everything tiny people need.

Both of our emotional experiences made sense.

And they were both optional.

When I really internalized the idea that all of my emotional safety and all of my financial security and all of my purposeful decision making actually resided with me, the only thing left to sort out was whether I thought our relationship was worth the effort it would require to dig in and discuss the nuances of our new "normal". We both dreamed of a flexible lifestyle with luxurious amounts of time to be with our kids and make memories together. We also wanted to grow our individual careers and stay connected to each other as a couple. A lot of the time, putting all of that together seemed unlikely, if not impossible.

Which left us with a choice to make.

Are we going to go hard in training for the SuperBowl or take a rest on the bleachers?

Honestly, it depends on the day.

Sometimes the bleachers seem pretty tempting. It's not so bad to be together exactly as we've always been.

Lots of other times the sparkliness of my dream marriage is enough to get me out on the field, running drills again. He's cute. He's fun a lot of the time. I have a very attractive vision of us enjoying our lives together in a connected way that we aren't experiencing as often as I'd like to just yet. So I hold on to that vision, using it as a motivation to take BIG risks in the way I talk to him, in the way I advocate for myself and in the things I allow myself to believe are possible for us.

I'm willing to flirt with him, even when the distance seems to stretch between us. I'm willing to ask for what I need, even though I know he might not comply. I'm willing to comfort myself when he doesn't and then reconnect with him to figure out why he didn't reciprocate my bid for connection. I'm willing to be vulnerable and open in asking if there are other ways to get me what I need from us because I believe that I'm worth getting what I really want.

Sometimes that process really, really sucks.

I have to be willing to hear things that don't feel amazing. I have to consider potentially painful truths about the way I'm showing up (or not) for us. I have to feel whatever I feel while I see him pulling back from me. I have to hold me when he doesn't and consider leaning into him when I really don't want to.

All of it's a risk. There's no guarantee that things will turn out well.

But it's also a risk to stop trying. And that risk DOES come with a guarantee that you'll continue having the relationship you really don't want. So, consider risking your current marriage in favor of pursuing the marriage you really, really want.

Maybe that new marriage will be with your current husband.

Maybe not.

That's 100% your call.

Just know that no matter which guy you end up with, the factor that'll determine the type of marriage you live in is YOU. Always. Do yourself the favor of telling yourself that truth. No matter what husband is doing, if you think it's impossible to ever have it any other way… then impossible it will likely be.

By requiring yourself to dream on purpose, you can change that whole "impossible" thing whenever you want.

Promise.

Allow yourself to dream big over the course of your lifetime and then commit to stretching your "normal" in small, purposeful, consistent ways on the daily.

It's hard work.

It might also be worth doing.

Whaddaya think?

One of the common roadblocks I see women lay down in front of themselves on the path they really want to be walking is the belief that "husbands don't change." If you believe that, you're gonna make it come true every time. So take care to be precise in the way you talk to yourself about possibilities and changes.

It's absolutely true that you can't change him.

Only he can do that.

But… you can influence him. It's completely in your control to sell him on what's best for you both. Especially when you do it from a place of confidence and excitement, which makes the whole interaction a much different experience than nagging or criticizing would be, because nagging and criticizing come from a place of doubt and hurt and disappointment.

Nagging happens when you doubt you'll get the life of your dreams.

Criticizing happens when you think that's your husband's fault.

All of that makes sense.

And none of it has to continue unless you want it to.

When you're operating from a genuine interest in improving your relationship and a solid love for the both of you, your efforts won't feel naggy or critical and here's why:

1. You are telling the whole truth as you go
2. You are working together to create something that he ultimately wants too

It's a partnership, not a manipulation.

Everyone can change when they see a good reason to do so.

Your job is to help make that reason crystal clear, without judging or blaming husband as you go. Sounds like: *"We both want the same thing (a connected, fulfilling relationship). Let's figure out how to make that happen. I'm thinking we would have a more fulfilling relationship if we invented a new way of operating here that works FOR us. You in?"*

When you believe it's possible for everyone to get what they want, the stakes feel lower and the need to compete subsides. The absence of urgency creates space for creativity which makes improving your marriage a fun puzzle for the two of you to solve together. All of that starts with you cultivating your awareness of what you don't believe is possible, questioning yourself about whether you want to believe a lack of possibility is true and then opening your mind to the idea that you might be wrong about your limitations.

From there, you ask directly for what you want - knowing that a "no" means nothing until you decide to accept it as a final answer. If you're not ready to let go of the thing you really, really want, consider the idea that a "no" is really a "not yet". All it means is that you've got some tweaking to do in your presentation. Take it as an opportunity to get to know your husband even better. Why exactly did he say no? What would make your request a super easy sell for him? How can you explain it in a way that makes saying yes the obvious option because you've so clearly outlined the benefits of your genius plan? This process requires you to not believe your brain when it tells you he's an unmovable bully who is only there to crush all of your dreams.

Let's look at a couple specific scenarios.

Just for practice.

> **Scenario 1:** You really want to take a woodworking course and you're pretty certain that your husband won't think it's a worthwhile investment.

Pitiful pitch - You: "*So, uh. I've been meaning to talk to you about something. And I know it's kind of expensive. I haven't ever tried it, but I think it could maybe be fun and possibly a really good thing for me. It's a woodworking course. I'll only be gone two nights a week and it's just for six months. I kinda like making stuff and I don't think I'll have too much homework to do. What do you think?"*

Him: "How much is it?"

You: (braces for impact) "A lot."

Him: "Nah. I don't think so. Not right now. We've got the deck. And Junior needs braces..."

You feel your heart sink. You grit your teeth to hold back your hurt and frustration. You decide it'll always be like this and you'll never be able to get what you want while he's in the way. Resentment creeps up and your connection to husband crumbles just a bit more. Your painful belief that he doesn't support your dreams is further entrenched.

But what if you tweaked your approach... even just a little?

Savvy Sales - You: "You know how I'm so awesome at making decorations and how I can put together pretty much any piece of furniture? I love that about me. I'm also ready to enhance my skills and make woodworking more than just a hobby. There's a class I want to enroll in, it costs $1500 and we can easily swing that with our current savings. I know you might be worried about me being gone. I totally get that because I love being here with you all too. It's just two nights a week for six months and it's really important to me. I have been looking for a creative outlet and this is it. What can we do to make this work?"

Hexagon Side Three

Him: "Gosh. That'll be a pretty big change for all of us."

You: (resist the temptation to interpret his comment as a lack of support) "You're right. It will be. And part of that change will be a more relaxed and fulfilled version of me, which is really a win for everyone."

Him: "$1500?"

You: (still not taking his comments personally or making them mean it's a no) "Yes." (smiles and adds) "And I'm worth it."

Him: "You are. Definitely. It's not really about what you're worth. I'm just not sure now is a good time."

You: (hanging on to full belief in what you deserve) "Tell me more…"

From there, you'll hear his side and incorporate his needs and concerns - without abandoning your needs and concerns - to create a plan that works well for the both of you. It may take some doing and you'll probably feel uncomfortable along the way. Just remember, that you're going to feel uncomfortable either way: uncomfortable as you long for something you aren't allowing yourself to have or uncomfortable as you figure out how to strengthen your collaboration skills and negotiate to land on a solution that serves you both.

Scenario 2: Husband delivers a consequence in a way that you believe is too harsh and loud and scary. You understand that he wants to redirect your son's behavior. You also think that he can do it in a better way.

Pitiful pitch - *You: "Hey! What the heck are you doing? Can't you see that you're scaring him? (pull son close to your side) I'm not going to let you talk to him that way. You need to get a grip and take a break. No one wants you around when you act that way."*

Him: "Oh okay. Go ahead and coddle him."

You: "I have to. Somebody needs to make up for how mean you are."

You want to protect your son. Of course you do. You also want to have some harmony in your home and you believe that's possible, even when you have to do the hard parenting work of delivering consequences. You hate how your husband is handling things and you feel you have to shut the interaction down at any cost - even if that means putting distance between you and your husband.

I hear you.

Safety matters.

100%.

And you can get it in a variety of ways. Here's another option you might want to try:

Savvy Sales - You: "Looks like there's an issue here. I'd love to help you if I can. (motioning to the other room) "Can we sidebar for just a quick sec?"

Him: (purses lips and glances between you and son) "Okay. But make it
fast." (thrusts a finger at son) "You stay right here."

You: "No problem. (in the other room) Loop me in with what's going on."

Him: (in a heightened, angry tone) "Joseph is being blatantly disrespectful. He knows what he's doing and I'm taking his video games away for the rest of the weekend. What's the problem with you? Why am I in here?"

You: "Okay. I hear you. And I want to help you two keep a good relationship if we can. I think yelling at him like that is just gonna push you two apart and I know you don't really want that. I get why you want him to respect you and I think the best way to get that done is to make sure he understands what the problem is. I'm not sure he does right now."

Him: "Oh. He does."

You: "Maybe. Maybe not. I still think it'd be helpful to explain again. Will you double check?"

Him: "Fine."

I know you might be thinking, "Yeah. Sure. That might work if he's willing to stop yelling and listen to me." And you're right. He might not. But even if he doesn't, you still have options for savvy selling. Might sound like this:

You: "Looks like there's an issue here. I'd love to help you if I can. (motioning to
the other room) "Can we sidebar for just a quick sec?"

Him: "No. We're in the middle of something here."

You: (relaxing your shoulders and breathing deeply on purpose) "Okay. That's fine. I'd still like to know what's going on, so I can help support you both if I can."

Him: "We're doing fine. Just stay out of it. Your meddling is making it worse."

You: (choosing not to be offended by what could be perceived as an attack) "I hope not. I really want to make it better and this doesn't feel great to me. I know you love Joseph and I know he's made some choices you don't like. Could you clarify for us both so we know what you want to be different?"

At this point, husband may or may not comply. Either way, you still have a choice to make. If he agrees to clarify, you can then continue helping the conversation move forward as clearly and kindly as possible. If he decides not to clarify and keeps blowing you off, you can choose to step back and see how his strategy plays out. You could also decide to de-escalate things by removing yourself and your son from the conversation or the room if you think that's what's best for everyone - including your husband - all the while expecting that he probably won't like it if you do.

I'm not saying that'll be pleasant or easy.

I'm just saying that you'll gain trust with yourself when you follow your gut. You'll also step a little closer to the marriage dynamic you want to have when you stop unconsciously following along with the old rules of "normal" that you really don't want to keep.

If you find yourself making pitiful pitches instead of savvy sales as you test out new kinds of "normal", not to worry. We've all done it. There's nothing wrong with you. It's just part of learning a new skill. Besides, none of us make our best choices when we are feeling threatened or sad or tired or unsure. Give yourself a break AND commit to getting so good at savvy sales that they don't require a ton of effort anymore.

To help you get ideas for how to successfully pitch what you really want, pay attention to how your husband advocates for himself. My guess is that he comfortably states what he wants to have happen with full expectation that it'll come to be. It's not that he's a pompous jerk who doesn't care about what other people need or want. I mean, I suppose that could be the case, but it's more likely that he was simply socialized, from a very young age, to believe that he deserves what he wants. Most men have always been taught, implicitly and explicitly, that their needs and wishes matter and would, of course, be met. It's not their fault. And that doesn't have to mean that your needs and wishes matter less.

It might mean that you have to do a little more mental pep talking than he does. Which, I know, can be kind of a drag. Also, remember that focusing on the unfairness only entrenches the unfairness further. Staying hurt over how you were raised differently than he was means you aren't spending time adopting the beliefs that were handed to him as he was growing up. And you could adopt those beliefs if you want to. You could decide to expect that your wants matter and effort should be made to bring them to life. It's your option to purposefully spend your effort learning how to comfortably self-advocate instead of bemoaning the fact that it's something you might not have been told how to do as a little girl. You can get curious about whether or not you believe you can ask for the rules to be bent or broken. You can notice when your guilt stops you from asking for something that might inconvenience someone else.

Maybe you change your approach when you notice those

things.

Maybe you don't.

The point is, the more often you choose to notice the ways you're holding yourself back, the more often you can choose to cut it out if you want to.

Some people might call you "bitchy" or "bossy" when you do.

Those people are wrong and you don't have to believe them. And the less we women believe them, the more likely it'll be that our daughters and their husbands will have less learned inequality blocking their path to a long and happy partnership.

It's also important to consider that while husband was more than likely socialized to believe he deserves exactly what he wants and was fed messages that supported him in taking up space in his world, he was probably also taught not to need support or appear weak in any way. Because of that conditioning, it's common for husbands to respond to something that seems scary or unfamiliar with what appears to be a non-negotiable hard pass.

Of course that's the case.

Because if it's "normal" for husbands to be the rock and the strength in the home, it makes sense that they would want to hold pretty firm boundaries to block out the unfamiliar. So when it seems like he's just saying no to EVERYTHING, that might be coming more from risk management and less from ruling with an iron fist. So try out making room for his weaknesses and vulnerabilities. Be willing to openly discuss his fears and doubts. When you do, you'll help hand him back his confidence and make it that much easier for him to say yes.

I've got a dream that husband and I will one day be the kind of couple who fluidly runs my business as a united, creative team.

That is not the case today.

The way I see it, he tends to overshare his opinions on

business strategy. I tend to interpret all of that as him talking down to me. So our painful "normal" spins and spins, keeping us shut out from the dream scenario I crave.

At least for now.

I'm still training for the SuperBowl on that one, though.

Don't you worry.

Just for funsies, I'm gonna share how one of my training drills went down: I opened up to husband about a decision I was making in my business and as per usual he started a long, drawn-out oration that involved talking down to me about a business concept that I'm already familiar with.

(Can you spot my not-so-helpful-normal in there? Do you see how I'm not quite telling myself the truth and am instead believing myself about some unflattering interpretations?)

As he spoke, I felt my temper flare. Doesn't he know I've read all the same books as him? How dare he think he can teach me about being an entrepreneur when I've made $450k over the life of my business and single-handedly supported our family through the global crisis of an out-of-nowhere pandemic?

Clearly, I had the option to rail on him for "mansplaining". It'd be pretty easy to make a solid argument for why I'd be totally justified in shutting down his spiel.

But...

Making justifications for choices that separate us won't really make me feel better given that my goal is for us to be more united about my business. Justifications don't get me to a connected, supportive marriage. Justifications only give me a "good" reason to feel bad.

No thanks.

Not this time.

Since I'd been allowing myself to dream about the way I

wanted us to work in my business, I had some familiarity with the vision of what that could be like. I'd imagined having a supportive, mutually beneficial brainstorming session with my husband. I'd daydreamed about what it might be like to live as the woman who consistently conversed with her husband in that way. Clearly, it'd be more strategic for the dream I'm pursuing to respond to his comments from that lady's perspective. She has what I want and thinking about her helps me know how best to respond to him on my way to becoming her.

She told me that if I want the kind of marriage where he and I work collaboratively on my business, I might want to entertain the idea of being confused instead of offended. I could decide it was strange for him to overexplain without deciding he was being rude. That decision would put me in an emotional state where I could more easily bring up my irritation in a calm, curious way and invite both of us to stay engaged in the discussion.

She also said it was fine for me to do all that after I took a grocery run to help me shake off my current self's gut reaction to be offended, cut him off, dismiss his comments as unsolicited and stomp off to make a decision all on my own.

I'm still a newbie at this skill after all.

Gotta pace myself.

The version of me who is living in the marriage I want is willing to slow things down, assume good intentions from husband AND share her preferences about the type of input that is the most welcome and the easiest to receive. She expects that he might have some push back and she also knows that she is worth the effort it'll take to co-create a working communication style.

See how the future version of you, who has the marriage you want, is an invaluable resource in helping you develop the stamina to weather the rumble until you and husband figure each other out?

Thanks, future you.

You can only access that wisdom if you are willing to see her in your mind's eye.

You can't see her unless you are willing to dream.

Unless you are willing to consider that the things you think are impossible now, might not actually be so.

Future you, the one who has the marriage you want, knows - for 100% sure - that her safety and success don't come from husband. She knows that she creates those things (or not) herself. Because of her faith in herself, she can make purposeful, calculated, and strategic decisions about putting herself out there - in emotional harm's way - because the bliss of her dreams is worth the anguish and grief that pave parts of the road from here to there.

Though many people might tell you they are, painful feelings don't have to be a reason to stop doing something that you really want to do. Joyce Meyer points out that, *"We often spend more time in relationships trying not to be rejected than we do building healthy connections."*

Why do we do that?

Because we are afraid. Plain and simple.

It's okay that we are. Our brains are wired to protect us from perceived threats.

Fear gets that job done.

Also useful to consider is the idea that you might be wrong that perceived rejection is the danger you might believe it to be. What if the most dangerous thing is actually you rejecting the marriage you really want because you haven't yet figured out how to help yourself through the pain of getting there?

It's your option to be someone in the now that your future self will thank you for later. By showing up with honesty and courage in your relationship, you'll teach yourself that you are totally capable of handling all of the emotions you once believed would stop you in your tracks.

Good news is: you're stronger than your painful story.

I am certain that's true.

Embracing that strength, even when it doesn't feel amazing, is how you'll get your marriage to expand to become the dream relationship you've always wanted.

You can survive your very worst emotion.

When you know that, you'll take more risks. And you'll get more rewards.

Every time.

Take Responsibility without Taking Blame

"The lesson I've learned most often in life is that you're always going to know more in the future than you know now."

- Taylor Swift

Hexagon Side Four

Take Responsibility without Taking Blame

For most of my marriage, it was REALLY important to me that my husband understand where he went wrong so that he wouldn't make the same mistakes again. I believed that if he didn't recognize that he'd made a mistake, there was very little chance that anything would change.

And I really wanted things to change.

So I kept pushing for him to admit fault.

As you might imagine, this didn't turn out very well.

Even though I kept at it for years.

If you've been hanging out in the self-help world for long, you've likely heard of the shame-blame trap. Here's how it goes: you notice something you don't like and then blame your husband for causing a problem. He creates some shame for himself with his thinking and then doesn't want to feel shame anymore, so he pushes back with a counter criticism about what you're doing "wrong". You then create some shame for yourself with your thinking. Of course, *you* don't like that feeling either, so you clap back with more blame for him and on and on it goes...

Might look like this in real life: You notice that husband used up the last of the butter and didn't put a new stick in the butter dish. You call him out, blaming him for only thinking of himself. Consciously or not, he agrees that it would have been nicer to replace the butter so he gets a twinge of shame. Shame is no fun, so he tries to dispel it by calling you a nag. You, on some level, start to wonder if he's right. Maybe you are too picky. Maybe it isn't that big a deal. Because of the way you're wondering about yourself, you feel some shame of your own - which isn't pleasant at all - so you deflect it by blaming him for his complete lack of self-awareness and his failure to take accountability.

And so it goes. You get the idea.

Both of you go round and round trying to displace the uncomfortable sensations in your body by making the issue the other person's fault.

Sound familiar?

Unless you're still on your honeymoon (and maybe even then), I'm guessing it does.

There's nothing wrong with you if that's the case.

Your human brain is simply trying to mitigate what it believes to be a threat.

All we've gotta do now is slow down and unpack what's going on.

You ready?

To make things even more clear, let's conceptualize the shame-blame trap as being like a see-saw you might see on a playground. You're sitting on one end and husband's on the other. You each take turns pushing against the ground, thus sending your beloved spouse on a bouncy ride that tosses them up and down without ever getting either of you to a useful destination.

One of my colleagues, Kara Lowentheil, teaches that the shame-blame see-saw rests on the fulcrum of "something's gone wrong", meaning that the only reason you get on that ride at all is because you are believing that something tragic has happened and you're not quite sure who should be fixing it or if it's even possible to make the repair.

Read that again: you're not quite sure who should be fixing it or if it's even possible to make the repair.

How do you feel when you read that sentence?

I'll wager a guess that it's some version of fear.

All human behavior is driven by variations of love and fear. Fear tends to bring out our less than ideal behavior because fear feels urgent and doesn't allow much time for research or space for rational

Take Responsibility without Taking Blame

thinking.

That's a terrific thing if you are evading a home invader or dodging a speeding car, because in life-threatening situations, quick action keeps you alive.

It's less terrific if you are trying to get along with your husband, because in close, personal relationships, quick action more often leaves you dead in the water.

Fear really wants you to zoom in on the threat. When you are zoomed in with tunnel vision, you ignore anything other than your desire to take the threat down and restore your sense of safety.

That's how blame is born.

Blame demands that someone admit something awful happened because of what they said or did. It sounds like: *"I really screwed that up."* or *"I should have known better."* or *"I can't believe that I was such an idiot."* or maybe even *"I don't deserve to be in this relationship at all because of what a mess I've made of things."*

Check in with yourself right now.

How do you feel after reading those statements?

Imagine how you might feel if you believed them about yourself day in and day out.

Not so great, right?

Of course it's true that piling on blame with those painful thoughts won't lead to anyone's best or most resourceful behavior. That's why taking responsibility will always be a more productive path than assigning or accepting blame. Taking responsibility sounds like this: *"Huh. I really didn't expect that to turn out that way. Didn't see it coming at all. Now that I know, I'll do X to make amends and put Y in place to avoid similar issues like this down the road."* Might also sound like: *"Oh wow. I'm really not clear on how this went down that way, but what I can tell you is that I would never want you to feel X way or have to deal with Y obligation. I love you and I'd be interested to know more about how I can contribute to things going better in the future."*

How do you feel after reading those statements?

Probably more open, more curious, more collaborative. Less defensive.

Probably.

Let's try it out with the butter example:

Coming from your mouth to his ears, blame sounds like: *"You're so selfish. You never think of what anyone else might need. I can't count on you for anything."* From there, shame rattles around in his head like: *"I'm such an idiot. I always forget really simple things. Why can't I be more thoughtful?"* Of course he doesn't like entertaining painful thoughts like those, so he sends the cycle round again.

Coming from his mouth to your ears, blame sounds like: *"You're such a nag. It's not that big of a deal. Stop overreacting."* Now it's your turn to create some shame with this internal dialogue: *"You're so hard to please. Why can't you just pick up the slack for him? No one likes to be around someone who's so irritable all the time."*

At any point, you could interrupt the cycle by taking responsibility and saying something like: *"I would really prefer that you refill the butter when you use it up. If you don't, I tend to use that as proof that you don't care about me which makes it hard for me to be patient with you forgetting. I'm asking you to remember and I'll try to look at it a different way if you forget again next time. Love you."*

Taking responsibility means you tell the whole truth, advocate for what you need and do your part of the work to make what you need happen.

It's also true that, at any point, he could interrupt the cycle by taking responsibility and saying something like: *"I would really prefer if you'd remind me about stuff like this in a kinder way. I really didn't realize not filling the butter would inconvenience you and I'm sorry. I never want you to think I don't care about you. That's not what forgetting means to me at all. I'm asking*

Take Responsibility without Taking Blame

you to consider that you might have it all wrong when you think I don't care and I'll do better with replacing the things I use. Love you."

Taking responsibility means he tells the whole truth, advocates for what he needs and does his part of the work to make what he needs happen.

Now, will he do all that?

It's hard to say.

Taking responsibility does require more presence of mind and purposeful word choice than hurling the barbs of blame.

So he might not do it.

Of course, you can hope that he will. You can even ask him to.

I would if I were you.

Marriage is so much easier if you're both actively looking for ways to get out of the shame-blame trap.

Also, know that you can't ever be sure about whether he'll take responsibility and work with you to regain closeness.

Most likely scenario is that sometimes he will and other times he won't.

Just like you sometimes take responsibility and other times don't.

Good news is, his behavior isn't really the point.

The more important question is: will YOU do all that?

I'm not asking because I want to let him off the hook. Because there is no hook. There's only two people creating their unique experiences while they live in the same space. When you tell yourself you have to wait for him to expend the effort to take responsibility before you can feel better, you're signing up for a roller coaster ride that you may not enjoy.

You're also not really taking much responsibility yourself.

So, consider the idea that you forever retain the opportunity to purposefully take responsibility *for you*. You always have the option to make choices that support your goals - regardless of whether he does the same.

I know that might sound like you're doing him a favor. And you are in a way.

He gets the benefit of living with someone who is in charge of her brain.

Lucky him.

You, however, get the way bigger, much more amazing benefit of BEING someone who is in charge of her brain. When you are in charge of your brain, you can create anything you want in your life. Really. It's true. So thank yourself often for giving you that gift.

Important to note is, being in charge of your brain doesn't mean you're never gonna get bugged ever again. When you take charge of your brain, you will still feel disappointment and loneliness and uncertainty. Because you're a human and that's part of the deal. Being in charge of your brain gives you the benefit of understanding *why* you feel those things - pssst… it's because of the story you're telling. When you understand that the story you choose drives everything else in your life, you then also understand how to reclaim your power and create a new feeling for yourself whenever you decide you want to (and only if you decide you want to).

Even if husband doesn't change a thing.

Go. You.

Remember, the shame-blame see-saw rests on the fulcrum of "something's gone wrong", meaning that the only reason you get on that ride at all is because you are believing that something tragic has happened.

Consider for a minute that you might be wrong in your assessment of "tragic-ness".

Consider also that being wrong here might be excellent news.

What if an empty butter dish is just an empty butter dish and

Take Responsibility without Taking Blame

not a clandestine commentary on the state of your relationship?

Notice how looking at it that way releases a lot of the emotional charge you'd previously assigned to an empty - and greasy - piece of porcelain. Then notice how empowered you feel when you tell the story exactly like it is without embellishment. Tune in to how ready you are to purposefully decide your next steps when you aren't distracting yourself with unconfirmed details.

Hello, Authority.

Glad to see you again, Power.

Even if the empty butter dish was, in fact, meant as a targeted slight, it's an option to remember that pain was always meant to be a part of our Earth experience. We can feel the pain without also believing that it isn't supposed to be there. When we know pain is an inescapable part of the human condition - especially when we are trying to interact with another human in close quarters for extended periods of time - there isn't as much need to push back against the pain. And when the need to push back isn't there, the ability to push forward remains.

I know it may seem like it's necessary to hold someone's feet to the fire when things go south, but what if it isn't? What if holding someone's feet to the fire might get you the behavior change you seek - at least temporarily - but could also torch the emotional connection you once had with him (and used to have with yourself) in the process?

Might not be worth it.

Or maybe it is.

That's your call.

When something in your marriage seems amiss or needs fixing and you choose to believe the problem shouldn't be happening at all, you're much more likely to feel some version of fear. To illustrate, let's look at the example of a baby teething.

Teething HURTS.

Babies cry.

NO ONE responds with, "Oh my goodness. How could this happen? We've gotta make it stop!" If we responded that way, all parents would be terrified through the first couple years of each child's life. We'd feel desperate and out of control and probably do some things that don't match up with our best selves.

But most of us expect the pain of teething as part of human development, so we retain our sense of control and are unlikely to freak out when we see Junior's swollen gums. We may sort of passively question the teething process and tongue-in-cheek wonder if God could have invented a better way to make teeth happen, but we are less likely to actually go on a wild, defensive crusade to make teething stop altogether. We know it's coming and so we get ready to ease the baby's suffering with cold, chewy things and medicine and snuggles. Because we accept that teething is supposed to happen, we spend very little time trying to prevent it or change it. We anticipate it, stock up on comfort tools and fearlessly love our littles through it.

We don't blame ourselves or the baby because teething isn't our favorite thing.

Instead, we take responsibility for handling teething like a boss.

It's our option to view the challenges of married life through the same lens we use for teething.

Most of us don't take that option, but what if we did?

If marital scuffles were openly acknowledged to be as non-threatening as teething, it's likely that we'd move through them more easily, feeling more curiosity and confidence as we go. We'd spend very little time trying to prevent them or change them. We'd anticipate them, stock up on comfort tools and fearlessly love ourselves through it all.

But when we see marital scuffles as a crack in the foundation of

Take Responsibility without Taking Blame

our very security, of course fear brings out the desperate, knee jerk response of grasping for control - often in the form of finding and busting whoever it is that's to "blame".

Sometimes we think that's him.

Other times we think that's us.

Either way, blame keeps us stuck on a painful see-saw ride that fixes nothing and serves no one.

Love - for you and for him and for the "us" you've created - makes room for the pain to be present without the need to lay blame.

Love - for you first - supports you in taking responsibility for telling the truth about your pain and also figuring out how to heal. Taking responsibility means owning the idea that you deserve to get what you need. It means recognizing your power to make your needs happen. It means accessing your options over and over until you get what you need done.

Many women don't do very much of that.

Instead, they approach their marriage from a disempowered place where they basically take what they can get. They figure out how to smooth things over and make the best of it.

It's not our fault that we do this.

Somewhere along the way, in some form or another, most of us were taught some version of the idea that husbands are in charge of most things while wives are in charge of ensuring that everything works out well.

However, there will inevitably come a time where things don't work out well. It'll be tempting in that moment to blame husband and try to change him. Or maybe you'll blame yourself and try to change you instead. As you've likely experienced, trying to change someone almost always results in distrust and contention between the two of you.

Between you and husband.

Between you and you.

Either way, disconnection rarely leads to lasting improvement.

This is the point where my clients usually ask me something like: "But... if I'm not trying to change him... then... I just have to put up with whatever he hands me?"

I hear that.

I know it might sound like I'm saying your husband can just do whatever he wants.

And... I kinda am saying that.

What I'm also saying is: *so can you.*

It's factually accurate that grown adults really can do pretty much whatever they want.

That's true for him.

That's true for you.

When you are hyper focused on the freedoms husband has, it can be pretty hard to see how you actually have all of those same freedoms too.

So now what?

Well... now you get to consciously choose between blame and responsibility.

Blame is confrontational and creates separation. Responsibility invites collaboration and connection because no one has to abandon themselves by admitting ill intent that probably wasn't there.

Maybe nothing's gone wrong if husband forgets to refill the butter.

And maybe nothing's gone wrong if you notice yourself feeling irritated when you discover that he did.

Maybe your irritation is there for a solid reason. Maybe its purpose is to alert you to a potential threat - just like the way your toddler points out scary shadows at bedtime, thinking there might be a monster in her room. When she shares her fears, you probably

Take Responsibility without Taking Blame

shine a light on the wall to show her that the shadow is being cast by her dollhouse and not by a monster at all. You hear her. You hug her. You don't make fun of her feelings and you take the time to show her what is truly scary and what doesn't have to be.

You can do the very same thing for your brain when she gets really busy warning you about various things. She's supposed to keep you alive, remember? That effort will, of course, include sending up alarm bells from time to time. Maybe even a lot of the time. You don't have to get annoyed with your brain for doing her job. You also don't have to think something's wrong with you when your brain does what she's designed to do.

Instead, you can consciously choose to shine a light on her thinking. You can lean in closer to discern if the threat she sees is real or not. Sometimes it will be. Often it won't. Being in charge of your brain helps you decide which experience to create for yourself by purposefully deciding what is truly scary and what doesn't have to be.

It really is an option to field the curve balls coming at your marriage without assigning ill-intent to husband or to yourself because those curve balls keep on flying.

One important exception would be if you genuinely believe your husband to be sitting back in a tall and spiky chair in his dark and foggy lair, tapping his fingertips together in evil satisfaction as he anticipates your fall.

If that's the case, you should run from that relationship.

I'll help you pack.

If it's anything less than that, it's your option to pause and get curious about what exactly went on. This is your chance to listen to the part of your brain that is pointing out scary shadows. She's warning you for a reason. Maybe she's telling you to high tail it out of there. Or maybe she's simply calling for you to stop hurting yourself by making the best of a set up that falls tragically short of meeting your needs.

As we discussed earlier, it's likely that your assessment of "tragic-ness" in your marriage will be exaggerated at times. Like when your husband forgets to refill the butter dish.

But other times?

Other times, your assessment will be spot on.

When I first started doing thought work, I was confused on this point.

I misinterpreted the concepts I was learning to mean that if I was in pain, well... then... it was kinda my fault for not managing my mind better. After all, I now knew that I had full freedom to think whatever I wanted to about anything my husband was saying or doing.

Back then, I was in pain a LOT of the time.

It's still true that I was in pain because of the story I was telling myself about the things going on in my marriage. That part will always stay the same.

The part I didn't know I could wiggle was the part where I added more pain to the pile by believing that I "should be" telling a different story.

In those early days, I developed a habit of blaming myself. Because it seemed like that's what I was "supposed to" do. I knew all about thoughts and feelings and how they were connected, so I thought I "should be" connecting them in a way that felt awesome - or at the very least, tolerable. I believed that if I'd connected my thoughts and feelings in a painful combination... well... that meant I was getting something wrong somewhere along the way.

It wasn't until years later that I clearly saw what was really going on.

Now I know that every time I told myself my pain was coming from my thinking, **and therefore my thinking must be flawed**, I was also forgetting that emotions are designed to bring us important, life-promoting information.

Information I shoved away for way too long.

All of that shoving kept me from advocating for myself as fiercely as I might have done otherwise. I was so busy telling myself that if I could really feel however I want to feel - no matter what he's doing - then my not feeling better was my fault and my fault alone.

Blame. Blame. Blame.

So painful.

Now I know that what I was thinking back then was true and not true.

I know that me not feeling better wasn't my fault, it was meant to be my fuel.

My fuel to hold myself more carefully.

My fuel to look at my life more closely. With more honesty.

My fuel to pursue what I want and need even more fiercely.

I want you to know all of that much sooner than I did.

I invite you to purposefully choose to spend as little time as possible rolling around in self-deprecating blame.

Sometimes your brain will send you there. It's probably a familiar road.

It's okay if you walk it sometimes. I do too.

All I'm saying is that maybe both of us could purposefully choose to look up from our habitual lives a little more frequently. We can cultivate our belief in our ability to make things better for ourselves. We can take responsibility for paying attention to the warning signs on purpose so that we don't end up stuck walking down the same old pathways of pain.

I know it might seem like ignoring your feelings helps you get along better in your relationships. Maybe you think holding things in helps you get more done in your day.

You might be right. That strategy probably works for a while.

But it won't work forever.

Because ignoring yourself inevitably comes with a cost.

As I mentioned, your emotions provide purposeful pieces of vital information. Just like the skin on your fingertips clue you in to the dangerous heat emanating from a stovetop, your emotions clue you in to the possibility of less obvious dangers entering your world. When you ignore your emotional cues, you lose the opportunity to evaluate their message and integrate that information into the decisions you make about your next steps.

Throwback to the first few years of my married life.

For a good chunk of that time, I wasn't managing my mind as well as I could have been, but not because I was thinking that some of husband's behavior was unacceptable.

I am fully aware that the word "unacceptable" is a thought.

I also know I could choose to tell the story a different way.

But... I don't want to.

I want to allow myself to confidently stand by my assessment.

So I do.

I've decided that "unacceptable" is the best, most fair thought for me to choose to describe some of the things that were going on back then. I will not make myself wrong for choosing that description. Because it seems exactly right to me. I feel that truth in my very bones.

So, when I say that I wasn't managing my mind as well as I could have been, I mean that I could have managed my mind much differently around the story I was telling about me and my power to influence the course of our relationship back then.

I made the mistake of thinking that my work was figuring out how to view my husband's choices in a more neutral way. How to contort myself into thinking that "nothing had gone wrong".

Take Responsibility without Taking Blame

When lots of things actually had.

Back then, his choices were not working for me.

I know it can be argued that "nothing had gone wrong" with his behavior. He's an adult man who can really and truly choose to behave however he wants to behave. He's physically capable of doing so. He wasn't breaking the laws of the land, so he retained his freedom and personal agency. In that sense, you could say that "nothing had gone wrong."

Except, the part that HAD gone wrong was the part where I gave up MY freedom and personal agency. I confused myself into thinking that I had to make the best of things I really didn't want to make the best of.

Which was a lie.

You never, ever, ever have to make the best of anything. Not even one time. Your job is to take responsibility for listening to cues from your body and brain to help you make wise decisions around building the world that you really want to live in.

Even if he's not helping you out.

Especially if he's not helping you out.

Maybe that'll mean you leave him.

Maybe that'll mean you stay and stand firm in your resolve around what you will and won't allow to be part of your day and part of your world.

I have no idea which route will be better for you.

I do know that staying connected to yourself through everything that comes your way will give you the best, most solid foundation to make that decision.

The point is to take responsibility for creating all of it. Not because he "deserves" a break or because you're "supposed" to turn the other cheek.

Nope.

Not this time.

You take responsibility because it feels better to YOU to know that you are in the driver's seat of your life - every single time. No matter what kind of boneheaded thing your husband is doing that day.

Allow yourself to be angry or hurt if you are.

Listen to the reasons driving your anger.

Make time to explore the stories causing your hurt.

Do yourself the favor of noticing your gut response and then take responsibility to care for yourself in a way that makes the most sense to you. Even if your husband doesn't like it or your nana would disapprove.

When husband does something that isn't your favorite, you have scores of choices around how to respond. Your only job is to decide on purpose what you're going to do. As often as possible, take responsibility for creating connection, love and understanding between you and you. Then, if you want to, go ahead and offer connection, love and understanding from you to him if that seems like the purposeful thing to do.

Know that you can also create distance, distrust and disappointment if you want to.

On purpose.

Sometimes that experience will be exactly right.

Remember that you always have a good reason for everything you think, feel and do. Take responsibility for figuring out what your reasons are, then follow those reasons with courage and conviction.

And if you decide to choose the distance that comes with distrust and disappointment, be sure that you are choosing to put that emotional distance between you and him for reasons YOU like. Reasons that serve what you really want most. Because when you choose reasons YOU like, you won't have to also suffer from feeling

Take Responsibility without Taking Blame

distance, distrust and disappointment between you and you.
Nothing is worth that rift in your relationship with yourself. I promise you that.

Celebrate the 1%

"Your future growth and progress are based in your understanding about the difference between the two ways in which you can measure yourself: against an ideal, which puts you in what I call 'the GAP' and against your starting point, which puts you in 'the GAIN' appreciating all that you've accomplished." - Dan Sullivan

Hexagon Side Five

Celebrate the 1%

You know how Dads stereotypically stomp through the house turning off all the lights in empty rooms because "Somebody's gotta pay the electric bill?"

In my house, that's me.

Probably because I'm the one paying the electric bill.

Also, I fancy myself an environmentalist.

And - *Oh. My. Goodness. How hard is it to flip a switch?*

Seriously.

I started stomping around like that nearly a decade ago. And still… the lights in my house are on pretty much all the time. Especially the light over the kitchenette in our basement. Husband uses the kitchenette most. It houses his "secret" stash of Oreos and his wide variety of beverages. Both of our offices are in the basement as well, in Jack and Jill style bedrooms across from the kitchenette. Husband likes to take his work breaks in the kitchenette area. It's sort of his happy place. The spot where he keeps his "Dad-Joke-of-the-Day" calendar and his favorite mug. Works great for most things. Except, in order to turn out the lights in the kitchenette, you have to walk all the way around the bar's countertop to reach the switch.

So yeah… it's an inconvenient architecture flaw.

And husband tends to leave the lights on because of it.

Which… well… you already know how I feel about all that.

Have I talked to him about the lights?

Yes.

Was I collaborative and direct in my approach?

Only sometimes.

Has he started turning them off?

Rarely.

I could easily make the case that we aren't getting anywhere on this issue. It's tempting for me to assume that he doesn't respect me

79

or doesn't appreciate the income I earn since he's so willy nilly with his energy expenditure.

Could also be true that the light switch is just located in an inconvenient place and he simply doesn't think about it before he heads back upstairs.

That *could be* the end of the story.

I concede the possibility that him not thinking about the lights does not *necessarily* mean he isn't thinking of me. Or that he doesn't appreciate the money I earn.

I mean… it's *possible* that's the case.

Now, if I require the "lights off percentage" to increase before I'll allow myself to feel better about the way things are going between husband and I, I might be in for a pretty long wait. Because the lights and his respect for me are not connected in his brain.

No matter how connected they are in mine.

So, I've got a choice here. I can choose to measure "improvement" by how often he turns off the lights OR by the types of feelings I create for myself when he doesn't.

When all of this started, I created a very bitter sort of rage when I'd see the lights left on. I'd stomp down the stairs after everyone was in bed and bemoan my plight in having to make the extra trek when it would have been so easy for him to flip the switch on his way out of his office. I used to feel so sorry for myself that my thoughtless husband frequently left me with two undesirable choices: 1 - waste my energy flipping off the light switch (a job he should have done) or 2- leave the light on and waste my financial resources.

My story sounds plausible, right? It's really not hard to flip a switch.

Except, it is for him.

And I'm married to him.

I wanted to stay married to him, so it was time to get creative.

Telling myself that same sad story of him not caring about what mattered to me, over and over again, just led to deeper bitterness and heightened rage. I was getting pretty tired of feeling bitter rage at the close of my day, so I consciously chose to try something new. I made the decision to entertain the idea that maybe he just gets busy and forgets to turn the light off after work.

He's just distracted.

Maybe that's all there was to it.

I invited myself to purposefully believe that none of his light switching behavior was about me at all. And now, on most nights, I feel mild irritation instead of bitter rage as I trudge down the stairs to flip that pesky switch.

Is it perfect?

No.

But it *is* the 1%.

Purposefully allowing myself to celebrate my wins in 1% increments - like moving from bitter rage to mild irritation - is very fun. Because winning feels awesome. And when I feel awesome, I pull more awesomeness into my life and into my marriage.

Here's how it works: with full conscious intent, I tell a story about husband that doesn't hurt me: *He just forgot the light. Period. It's not my favorite thing about him, but I forget things too - so I get it. And none of that has anything to do with me.*

Then, I go on to tell a story that makes me look impressive.

Because I am.

Nice job, Candice. You are so understanding and patient and environmentally conscious. The planet and Husband are very, very lucky to have you.

Quick check in with you: If you felt weird or disoriented or giggled a bit while reading such a self-congratulatory sentence, I get it. Most of us women are chronically under-impressed with ourselves.

Chronically.

Under.

Impressed.

We tend to get all squidgy when someone gives us a compliment and we are certainly not in the habit of so openly claiming our fabulous qualities or inspiring accomplishments.

Why?

First, because most of us are taught to believe that we live life in a zero-sum game, meaning that if we own our unique amazingness, then we must be taking away from someone else's.

Second, humans also tend to be pretty afraid that other people might disagree with our self-congratulatory comments. So we don't make them because we don't want to appear foolish or be shot down.

I'm here to offer that maybe you don't have to be worried about either thing. Because the first one isn't true and the second one doesn't have to matter if you don't want it to.

The truth about human beings is that every single one of us is amazing without even trying. Case in point: we - all of us - take solid food, smash it with our teeth and use that mush to regenerate our bodies.

Ah. Maze. Ing.

But not only that, we also breathe and pump blood through our bodies without any conscious effort at all. We grow taller without thinking about it. We remember how to do basic tasks - like driving home or brushing our teeth - without specifically walking ourselves through a step-by-step instruction list.

All of it's a freaking miracle.

Now that we've established how every single one of us is limitlessly amazing, let's also consider how we all get things wrong, a LOT.

Like when you struggle to see your own impressiveness and instead beat yourself up over making a thoughtless comment or forgetting a commitment.

Like when other people are confused and think it's important to call attention to your shortcomings. Or when they misunderstand your good intentions.

It's not their fault if they don't easily see how amazing you are. When that happens, it simply means that they've got some sort of personal demon on their back or in their brain, so they aren't thinking straight at that one moment in time.

Doesn't have to be a big deal unless you make it into one.

You can forgive that person for being distracted and go on loving yourself fiercely anyway.

I suggest that you do.

Because loving yourself fiercely is YOUR job.

When you don't, that's not your fault either. You've also got some demons that climb onto your back or into your brain at times.

Doesn't have to be a big deal unless you make it into one.

You can redirect and go on loving yourself fiercely anyway.

Again, I suggest that you do. Because you teach everyone around you how to treat you by the way you treat yourself.

So treat yourself exquisitely well as often as you can.

Embracing the idea of 1% celebrations is a terrific way to treat yourself exquisitely well. Celebrating the 1% guides you to purposefully appreciate all the amazing things you're doing. The 1% practice helps you focus on all of the awesome things about your relationship.

Not because you are blind to the problems in your marriage.

Not because you aren't willing to work through your personal flaws.

Just because continuously and purposefully noticing the great things about you as a woman and about you two as a couple gives you a solid reason to do the work of changing the not-so-great things.

The first and best step is usually to change the not-so great dialogue going on in your own brain - like I did with the lights. From there, you can change the not-so-great things going on between you and husband by choosing self-supportive, slow-to-make-assumptions inner dialogue as often as you can.

When you purposefully train your brain to talk to you in that way, it's so much easier to stretch the space between what is happening in the world around you and ***how you respond to*** what is happening in the world around you.

That space is EVERYTHING.

It's where all marital battles are either detonated or disarmed.

The stretched out space sounds something like: *"Okay. X is happening. I'm thinking and feeling Y. A, B and C are my options. There are lots of ways I could take this whole thing and I'm not compelled to take any particular one. I'm in charge here. There's no rush."*

In every situation, the only expectations that exist are the ones you've adopted. Sometimes you'll be completely aware of your expectations. You'll know that you chose them on purpose because you've consciously practiced them over and over (ahem, turn off the light!).

Other times you might surprise yourself with what you're believing. In those moments, when you're dealing with unconsciously held rules for how things should be going, the stretched out space is even more important. That space is where you'll discover if you're seeing a "message" that isn't really there. It's where you'll learn to recognize the nervous chatter of a brain that's desperately warning you of "danger" when none actually exists.

Let's case study two seemingly small scenarios that could easily be misinterpreted as disappointments, but could be counted as hidden delights if the 1% rule is at play.

ONE: The UBER - There we were, husband and I, standing in the checkout line of the grocery store. As we waited, the conversation turned to discussing the logistics of the rest of our day. Dropping off the car to be serviced. Grabbing our youngest from daycare. Getting our oldest to baseball practice. Making sure we hit everybody's parent-teacher conference. All the little errands that make up our lives.

It soon became apparent that dropping the car off together (so the driver would have a ride back home) might clash with the time-sensitive task of grabbing our youngest from school. My brain then set out to orchestrate some scheduling acrobatics that would make everything work, but only if executed with the strategic precision of a seasoned black ops team.

Husband "solved" all that by offering to "just get an Uber".

An Uber? *An UBER?*

The exact same alarm bells that warn me about wasting resources by paying for left-on lighting went off again to warn me about wasting resources by paying for an Uber in our hometown.

Our. Home. Town.

Not on my watch.

I bristled.

So did he.

I believed he "wasn't respecting my effort" to bring in income.

He told himself that I "didn't think he was worth the forty bucks" it'd take to get him home from the mechanic.

My blood bubbled. His jaw clenched.

A standoff ensued.

Right there in the grocery checkout line.

And I let it be.

I left him with the cart and the debit card and walked over to the sliding doors that led to the parking lot, where I promptly began scrolling through random Facebook countdowns on my phone. I breathed deeply and watched myself experience what it's like to be offended.

I also narrated the whole thing inside my head.

Sounded something like: *"Okay. He's mad about something that isn't true. I'm thinking he's spending my money with reckless abandon and I'm feeling unappreciated. I could yell at him. I could cry. I could walk away. I could talk to him. Those are my options. There are probably lots of other ways I could take this whole thing and I'm not compelled to take any particular one. I'm in charge here. There's no rush."*

I took several more deep breaths and ran through all of that a couple more times while I waited for him to pay for our groceries and meet me at the door.

When he got there, I could feel that my blood temperature still lingered at lukewarm. I could see that his jaw continued to clench. On the way home, we tripped our way through a tense-ish discussion about what does and does not feel like support. It wasn't our favorite conversation, but we did keep conversing because both of us value the practice of giving and receiving respect in our marriage. Neither of us wanted to risk buying into an unkind message that our spouse wasn't sending. Instead, we both wanted to take the time to slow down and assess whether danger was even present in this conversation at all.

Even though it felt pretty terrible to do so, we talked it through to 90% resolution, which was different from how we might have ignored each other completely in days gone by. We did it because we wanted to practice keeping more open communication and less stone cold silence between us.

In that moment, our best effort turned out to be a pretty chilly chat.

It wasn't perfect.

Definitely just 1%.

But it's something.

In situations like these, something is almost always better than nothing. Especially because acknowledging the tiny somethings helps to keep us both committed to each other and to doing the work that we knew marriage would be.

TWO: The Book Writing Snacks - Fun fact: husband contributed to the creation of this book by continuously supplying me with snacks and drinks. Almost on the daily, he'd drop our youngest at preschool and then bring back some sort of provision to support me in getting through the next section of this work. Thanks husband.

Since I'm always trying to be extra, super clear about what works for me and what doesn't, I mustered the self-support to text him a specific cookie order: E.L. Fudge, NOT double stuffed, just regular stuffed. Plus Mint Milanos. As I composed the text, I promised myself that my request was not necessarily a burden and even if it was… my desires were worth it.

I wrote out what I wanted and sent it off, all the while feeling through the possibility that he might think I was picky or bossy or difficult because I'd said what I wanted right out loud.

1%.

Nice job, me.

Husband then came home with two packages of not-what-I-ordered cookies: Milk Chocolate Milanos + Grasshoppers.

Sigh.

Now I I had a choice to make. The decision making process sounded like this in my head: *Okay. He brought the wrong cookies. But he still brought cookies. I'm thinking that I'd prefer to have what I asked for. I'm feeling guilty because I think I should just take what I can get without throwing a fit. I could eat the cookies. I could put them in the pantry. I could throw them away. I could tell him what's up. There are probably lots of other ways I could take this whole thing and I'm not compelled to take any particular one. I'm in charge here. There's no rush."*

Historically, I would have simply thanked him and made the best of it. Cookies are cookies after all. It's not like the ones he presented were inedible or anything. I could enjoy them just fine if I wanted to. That's what an agreeable wife would do.

Except... I wasn't working toward being an agreeable wife.

The goal was to be extra, super clear.

I know it might surprise you to learn that it could ever be a challenge for me to be extra, super clear. If you've ever heard me speak, you'd probably guess that I'm very direct. I tend to get right to the point with humor and confidence and all that.

If something is a problem, especially a big problem, you'd be absolutely right in that assessment. I have pretty much no trouble calling out behavior that I perceive to be disrespectful or dangerous.

The trouble comes when someone has done something "kind" that is also "wrong."

Like bringing home cookies, but not the cookies I asked for.

Feels tougher to call that out.

Because I believe the intent was good. And I don't want to seem ungrateful.

Still, my goal of extra, super clear remained. So, I swallowed hard and took a breath. I purposefully chose to tell myself that correcting his mistake didn't have to mean that I didn't fully appreciate his effort.

1%.

"Husband," I said, *"I wanna tell you something and I don't want it to hurt your feelings. You game?"*

Because he's used to me saying that kind of thing, he offered full honesty back. *"I will certainly try, what is it?"*

I asked him if he was aware that E.L. Fudge was actually a flavor of cookie and was not, in fact, synonymous with the umbrella Keebler brand.

He confirmed his understanding and went on to say that he bought Milk Chocolate Milanos because the store was out of Mint Milanos. He then bought Grasshoppers as a back up mint-y option. He reasoned that maybe the two cookies together would make up what I originally ordered, then went on to say how he is familiar with E.L. Fudge because he'd purposefully set three of the little guys up - with candles on their heads - when he brought me breakfast in bed on my 30th birthday.

We laughed and reminisced and connected.

Even though I hadn't received exactly what I'd asked for.

1%.

Notice how neither of those scenarios seemed like a win at first. But when I dug in and made space for improvement to surface, it did.

Even though I didn't get every single thing I wanted in either case, in both cases I got enough of what I wanted to keep me going.

You don't have to wait to cross the finish line of your relationship goal to actively appreciate the strides you are making.

I encourage you to NOT wait that long.

Because celebrating as you go means you get to feel awesome more often. Feeling awesome then makes it that much easier to create the things you want to have in your world.

Know that winning in this way won't always feel like winning while you're doing it. Sometimes you'll still go to bed mad or hurting. The 1% win in that case is knowing that you're no longer lying to yourself about how you feel.

Sometimes the date night details won't quite pan out and neither of you will roll with it the way you really want to. The 1% win there might be openly acknowledging where things went awry or brainstorming together about a fix for next time.

Other times you'll hold his hand or receive his hug and notice that you don't feel as comforted by the contact as you expected you might be. In that scenario, 1% winning might be appreciating the intent of the gesture and staying with it while allowing yourself to acknowledge that the emotional component may take a little longer to catch up.

Joy in relationships and trust in your husband are learned skills. They take focus and effort and practice. Lots of purposeful practice. These skills also require you to weather the surprises that crop up along the way, unpleasant though they may seem at the time.

For example, purposefully telling the whole truth usually shifts a relationship's dynamic. When you start telling him the whole truth more often, it might seem like your connection becomes a bit less certain as you both recalibrate to this new level of openness. Similarly, when you start telling yourself the whole truth more often, you might find that you feel a little more guilt as you figure out how to balance your needs with the needs of your loved ones.

Good news is: when you start telling the truth more often, you'll also have more opportunity to celebrate 1% wins. So plan to purposefully notice the baby steps you're taking to get closer to the marriage you really want to have.

There will be lots of 1%, baby steps wins to celebrate.

I'm sure of it.

And they really do add up.

Taking a pause. Internally narrating what's happening between you and him before you decide how to respond. Allowing something to count even though it's not perfect. Saying no when you want to.

Saying yes when you want to. Not interpreting any of your emotions - or his - as emergencies. Telling a generous story about his intent. Acknowledging the kind motives in your heart. Hanging on to the vision of living in the marriage you always thought you'd have.

1% + 1% + 1% = meaningful change over the course of your life together.

Sounds like something worth celebrating to me.

It's natural for humans to focus on the negative. Doing so is actually an adaptive strategy designed to help keep us alive. However, if we aren't careful, the same adaptive strategy we use to keep ourselves alive can actually keep us from fully living.

We give up on our dreams.

We settle for things we don't really want. Then we look around and all we can see is how tough it feels to keep walking toward what we want when it seems like there is still so far to go.

Enter the 1%.

When you consciously celebrate how far you've come, that's when you'll muster the strength to go on persevering. When you purposefully pay attention to the things you know today that you didn't know yesterday, that's when you find motivation to keep on keeping on.

It can be so helpful to consider that progress has less to do with time passing and more to do with the small decisions you make every day. Lasting change builds momentum as you commit to making quick, confident decisions over and over again. And if you celebrate those useful choices as you make them, you'll gain enthusiasm for the process and maybe even enjoy the experience as you go.

It can be really tempting to get distracted by your past self when things get tough. Watch for phrases like: *"We're never gonna get it right."* and *"I don't know why I thought this would ever be different."* Those are simply siren calls from your primitive brain, tempting you to save your energy and avoid anything new. Because "new" takes effort and your brain is designed to be an energy conservationist.

When your past self doubts the possibility of a less painful future, that's your current self's chance to remind your brain that you are purposefully spending energy on chasing the dream relationship you really want to live in.

You're actively challenging the story you've been telling about your marriage because you want a better story to be true.

Of course you're not fully there yet. This is the part where you're developing your relationship skills in grueling two-a-day practices in the sweltering summer heat. This is what will make you primed and ready for the big game a couple months down the road.

This part is tough.

On purpose.

By design.

Sticking it out through this part will strengthen your belief in yourself and show you how sweet it is to become the woman who can make your goals happen. So, take care to avoid getting distracted by what's gone on in your past. As C.S. Lewis famously teaches, *"Getting over a painful experience is much like crossing the monkey bars. You have to let go at some point in order to move forward."*

Every time you loosen your grip on the story you've always told about a marriage set up you don't really want is a call for celebration.

1% at a time.

Just as important as not getting distracted by the past is a commitment to not be discouraged when thinking about what's in the future. When you continuously notice all the ways your marriage isn't lining up with what you imagined it'd be, it can be pretty challenging to get up the gumption to keep moving forward. You then spend your present moments lamenting over how none of this was supposed to go that way - and you know what that does?

Loses more moments.

Piles up more regrets.

Pushes determination further and further out of the picture.

You deserve better.

Better happens by orienting to and celebrating the 1% progress as often as you can. Hang on to your determination in the present by focusing on how far you've come, not how far you still have to go. Make it a point to enjoy the progress you've made, no matter how tiny that progress may sometimes seem.

Then, do yourself the favor of allowing for a little bit of magic to make waves in your marriage. Even if you're only able to leave open a teeny pinhole of light in a thick wall of blackness, let that light in. Allow your brain to noodle on the idea that the Universe or God or energetic forces or spirit animals really do want what's best for you. Consider that you might not have to do everything all on your own to make your marriage more of what you want it to be. Crack open your perceptions just enough to let joy and magic and great delight find their way into your relationship. All you've gotta do is make space for them to join in.

Thomas S. Monson once said, *"Never let a problem to be solved become more important than a person to be loved."* When I first read that, I thought he meant I was supposed to love my husband above and beyond how much I would love a solution to a painful part of our marriage. I still think I'm correct in that interpretation. I also now know that he meant I'm supposed to love ***myself*** above and beyond how much I would love a solution to a painful part of our marriage. Feels so much nicer to include myself in that love fest. Of course it does.

So love the people - both you and husband - first and foremost.

As fiercely as possible.

Know that love doesn't mean you have to do anything. At all. Love simply refers to what you feel and how you think and what sort of stories you tell about your marriage.

Be sure you are telling those stories on purpose as often as possible.

Watch for and celebrate even the tiniest trickles toward change, trusting that solutions will come. Choose to celebrate the 1% starting right now. Plan to continue on all day. Every day.

Your future self, the one living in your uber-connected, totally fun marriage - thanks you.

Don't Believe Everything you Think

*"You either walk inside your story and own it,
or you stand outside your story and hustle for your worthiness."*
- Brene Brown

Hexagon Side Six

The first time I told someone she didn't have to believe everything she thinks, she laughed and softly shoved my shoulder. Then, she told me more painful details of the story that held her stuck in a place where she didn't want to be.

She thought I was making a joke.

But I wasn't.

I was trying to hand her the key to the universe.

I'm not upset that she didn't take it. It's really okay.

Most people believe **everything** they think, without a second thought. When they do, they cause themselves a lot of heartache. I've done it. You have too. Both of us will probably do it again. All of that is okay.

Really.

It's part of the human experience.

Also, I think it'd be useful for us to shine a light on some commonly believed pain points. Could be fun to remind ourselves of our option to stop believing hurtful stories.

Anytime we want to. And only if we want to.

> You game?

> Let's do it.

Below, you'll find my carefully curated list of the top 4 things I suggest you stop believing. None of them are true. All of them are painful. Even better, all of them are optional. You can drop any one of them whenever you want to - if you want to.

1. There must be something wrong with me

When women notice something isn't going the way they want it to in their marriage, they often choose to believe that something must be wrong with them. They then twist themselves in knots to primp more, cook more, clean more, listen more, do more, go without more, stifle themselves more, give of themselves more, accept more, forgive more… and on and on and on. It's pretty common for women to believe that if they just do or say or be infinite variations of "more", then everything in their marriage will finally turn around.

Don't get me wrong.

Sometimes there is more you could do.

Other times it'd be helpful if you did less.

The point is that, either way, it's never true that the problems you are experiencing in your marriage come from a fundamental flaw in you, as a person.

That's never the case.

Maybe you discover that there's something you want to do differently in the way you interact with him. Go ahead if you want to. Just know that doing the new thing won't change anything about how awesome you are as a person or how valuable you are in the relationship and to the world. You were awesome and valuable all along. That's true no matter what sort of thoughtless comment your husband or your mother-in-law offer up. It's true regardless of any insensitive behavior either one of them might display.

When someone acts harshly toward you or demonstrates a lack of patience with you, all that means is that something is going on for them. They are in some kind of pain and, in that one moment, they aren't handling their pain well.

Truly.

That's it.

What's very important to specifically highlight right now, is that no matter what anyone else implies or even directly says, no type of abuse, mistreatment or unkindness ever means ***ANYTHING*** about you.

Not ever.

Also, knowing that husband's behavior isn't ever about you

does not mean that you have to forgive anything you don't want to forgive. You're never required to smooth things over. You don't have to look the other way.

And you can, of course, forgive anything if you like. Especially when you remember that forgiveness comes in lots of flavors. You can forgive him and move on to a new life without him in it. You can forgive and stick around to figure it all out together. There are lots of options in between. No option is "morally better" than any other option. Each situation is unique and you are the best person to decide how you'd like to proceed.

No matter what you decide to do, please remember that none of his behavior is about you.

Not ever.

Consider also that sometimes it's you that's treating you harshly. Even then, that still doesn't mean anything about you. All that means is something is going on for you. You are in pain and, in that one moment, you aren't handling your pain as well as you could. You're simply taking it out on yourself instead of taking care of yourself.

Because you're a human. And you've likely been offered the idea that not letting yourself "off the hook" is the best way to get things done. Even though that strategy doesn't usually work long term.

Also, because you're a woman. And you've likely been taught that your needs are supposed to come last, or that you can meet your own needs, but only so you'll then be able to meet other people's needs even more efficiently. Neither of which are even true.

When you notice that you aren't handling your pain as well as you could, that's your opportunity to lean into your pain with love and understanding. You have a good reason for everything you do. Your job is to figure out what the reason is. It's your opportunity to discover what you need and then brainstorm how to get your needs met in a more useful, kinder way.

Remembering that you are inherently whole and infinitely valuable offers you the best set of mental and emotional resources to help you improve any situation you aren't in love with.

Note that I said: improve your situation, not increase your worth.

Because there is nothing wrong with you.

It's likely that the only thing "wrong" is that you've stopped loving and supporting yourself as solidly as you could. I know that's true because a well-loved, fully supported version of you will always seek after and create a best-case-scenario situation for everyone she cares about, including herself. She'll show up to her relationships with kindness and generosity because she's given kindness and generosity to herself first. When she does, everyone wins.

2. He hurts my feelings

I'm only including this one here because it's factually inaccurate to assert that husband is in charge of your emotional experience. Which is great news because we really don't want him to be. If he's like most humans, he has a hard enough time being in charge of his own feelings. It benefits no one to put him in charge of yours too.

Every person creates their own emotions. All the time. No matter what.

I know that you might not love this suggestion. In some ways, it seems easier to blame husband than it does to do the work of taking care of yourself.

To be fair, it's 100% true that some of the things he says or does will require more work from you than other things he says or does. If he'd toss his socks in the hamper or remember to pick your kid up on time or be nicer to your sister then you really would have fewer challenges to figure out. You're correct that when he doesn't do those things, it will probably take some effort to purposefully create your feelings - especially when you have a strong preference for some feelings over others. (more on this coming with painful thought number 3)

The fact that you are always in charge of your emotions is a fact that hands all of your power back to you.

He can't make you feel anything.

I promise you that is the case.

I also promise that you **want** that to be the case, because when you believe it is - you're back in charge. You no longer need to wait on him to do something different before you're allowed to feel the way you want to feel.

That's freedom.

Your feelings get hurt if you hear whatever he says, believe it and then turn his words into weapons to hurt yourself. Your feelings get hurt if you observe what he does, interpret it in a painful way and then believe yourself about your interpretation.

Those are the only two ways hurt feelings happen.

Truly.

You never have to believe what he says about you. Especially if it's mean. You never have to interpret his behavior in a way that feels awful to you. Especially if it's cruel.

Also, you can expect that you're going to believe him at times. Especially when he's mean. You're sometimes going to interpret his behavior in a way that feels awful to you, even if you try not to. Especially when it's cruel.

I know because I do it too. Even though I've been doing this work for years.

Right now, we're not going to focus any more time here because I anticipate that you might be tempted to use this little "he can't hurt your feelings" kernel of truth as a reason to blame yourself for everything, which will only add more suffering to your pain.

My clients do that all the time.

I've done it too.

Right now, let's do our best to circumvent that painful self-blaming and self-shaming experience if we can. We've acknowledged the pain that comes with believing he has the power to hurt your feelings. Next, let's move on to question a belief that's likely been hurting you even more.

3. I shouldn't care about what other people think/I shouldn't feel bad about what they say

First off, humans are a tribal species. We are programmed to notice and attune to what others of our kind are thinking and doing. From an evolutionary perspective, it was very wise for us to make sure our tribe accepted us because that meant they'd be more likely to share their food, make space for us by their fire and warn us if a saber tooth tiger looked ready to pounce.

Of course you care what other people think.

Especially husband.

Your brain is designed to guide you to pay attention to his opinion.

The part of that process that you can challenge, if you want to, is the part where you let his opinion dictate your behavior. Sometimes you'll want to let that happen. Other times you won't. It's not that you need to stop caring about what he thinks. The invitation is to simply become more conscious of how often you make choices based on what *he* thinks vs how often you make choices based on what *you* think.

In today's modern society with well-stocked grocery stores, HVAC systems and easy-to-install security cameras, you no longer have to rely on other people - not even husband - to ensure your survival.

Even so, you'll probably still feel yourself caring about what he thinks.

Of course you will.

You also have the option to remind yourself that his disagreement doesn't matter nearly as much as you might be thinking it does, because you are fully capable of ensuring your own survival and you are ultimately in charge of creating your emotional experience.

All day. Every day.

You're also allowed to logically understand the concept that he can't hurt your feelings and still create hurt, pain, fear, jealousy or disappointment for yourself when you interact with him.

Sometimes those emotions will seem befitting given what's going on in your marriage. You might want to feel hurt if he criticizes your work ethic. Disappointment might make sense if he's late for date night. And if you discover that he's been a little extra friendly with a gal at work, well - anger might be exactly right. Totally your call.

Emotions are information. They help clue you in to what you're willing to accept in your life and what you aren't. It's your option to recognize the emotion and listen to its message so that you can better organize your life in a way that fits best for you, your values and your goals.

If you feel hurt after husband criticizes your work ethic, it's possible that the hurt is there to remind you that you value respectful collaboration in your relationship. Hurt is telling you that respectful collaboration was missing from this particular interaction. Such a good thing to know. From there, you have the option to support yourself in requiring respectful collaboration and working with husband on how exactly you can bring more of that respect and collaboration back into your relationship. Thanks, hurt.

When you find yourself feeling disappointed while waiting for husband to show up on date night, it could be true that disappointment is there to reinforce your preference for clear scheduling updates and your desire for quality 1-1 time. Such useful data. You can use those data points to help you discuss scheduling strategies that are likely to produce the quality 1-1 time you've been craving. Much obliged, disappointment.

The anger churning in your stomach when you think about husband and the gal at work and whatever went down between them, might be there to warn you that your values have been violated. Anger is showing up strong to help you maintain the agreed upon boundaries you've established in your marriage. So nice to be reminded of exactly where those boundaries are. Even if husband decides he no longer wants to abide by those boundaries, anger still serves to clarify your preferences and helps guide you to make choices that comply with what you've decided to expect. Appreciate you, anger.

Your body is equipped to feel all these emotions. On purpose. All of these emotions, and countless others, show up to serve you in creating your very best life and your closest relationships.

What if I'm right about that?

I know you might be wanting to quote me some version of the tried and true "master of your emotions" or "bridle your passions" mantras.

I'm in.

Let's do that.

Because "bridle" means "tame" and "master" means "rule over." Neither of those words implies a ceasing or suppressing. If we bridle our passions like ranch hands bridle horses, that simply means that we figure out how to use the power of our emotions to create the lives we want. Just like ranch hands figure out how to use the strength of their horses to make ranch jobs easier to complete.

Ranch hands partner with their horses. In a relationship of

mutual respect.

What might it be like to do the same with your emotions?

When we believe that we aren't supposed to care what other people think or that we aren't supposed to feel bad about things they say, that's when we limit the power of the magical, game-changing emotion tools we've been given.

If you snap back at husband's comment about your work ethic in an unconscious effort to dispel your hurt feelings, you'll miss an opportunity to get to know yourself a little bit better.

If you brush your disappointment away when husband finally arrives for your date, you'll lose that chance to actively create more of what you need.

If you pretend that everything's okay on the outside while you're seething angry internally, you'll never get a clear idea of what your needs are or where your boundaries lie.

What a waste that would be.

Because you are someone worth getting to know.

Because your wants and desires are something worth creating.

Just like the sensations on your skin warn you to pull your hand away from the hot stovetop, your emotions warn you about situations that might get in the way of your dreams. When you listen to what your emotions are saying, you'll be more informed about how to proceed. Which likely means you'll be more successful in getting what you want.

So, why not open up to all of your feelings?

As a favor to you.

Let your emotions inform you about how and where your marriage matches up with your values, as well as where it doesn't. Use that information to adjust things as desired.

Humans are designed to experience all emotions.

I promise you that's the case.

Nothing is wrong with you or your life or your marriage if you sometimes feel icky.

Or crappy.

Or even terrible.

Judging yourself for feeling things that are supposed to be there only blocks you from accessing insight you were meant to have.

Telling yourself that you shouldn't care about what other people think or that you shouldn't let them hurt your feelings only invites you to abandon yourself even more.

None of that is necessary.

What you are feeling is exactly right, no matter what it is.

4. I don't know how any of this happened

When my clients start noticing improvements in their marriage, the most common response is bewilderment. Sometimes even straight up confusion. I ask them how those changes happened and, usually, they sincerely tell me that they do not know.

Because, as we discussed, most of us are chronically under impressed with ourselves.

Chronically.

Under.

Impressed.

Luckily, I always know. I remind them that they know too. It's just that they aren't used to knowing. The reason their marriage is improving is always the same: they created a different experience by purposefully telling a different story about how their marriage works and about what it means to be a wife.

Glennon Doyle describes something similar in her book, *Untamed*. People often tell her that she and her wife are very lucky to have the life they do. Here's how she responds: *"It's true. We are terribly lucky. It is also true that we imagined this life before it existed and then we each gave up everything for the one-in-a-million chance that we might be able to build it together. We did not fall into this world we have together now, we made it. I'll tell you this: The braver I am, the luckier I get."*

The same is true for you. And for me. And all wives everywhere.

The braver we are, the luckier we get.

For better or for worse, you did not fall into the relationship that you currently have with your husband.

You made it.

If you aren't loving the marriage you have now, I know that message might seem depressing. You can allow yourself a moment to sigh if you want to. Then, when you're ready, you can remember that you were doing your very best at the time with the information you had back then. Take heart in knowing that if you made the marriage you have now, you must be able to make a different marriage if you want to.

Because you, my friend, are a powerful creator.

Maybe you'll create a new, made-over marriage with the same guy. Or maybe you'll remake everything from scratch. Either way, you are in charge of the making. You could let that be a fun possibility. Or at least an intriguing one.

You created your marriage exactly as it is now.

You can create something different if you want to. You can create more of the same if you like the direction things are heading. Or maybe you'll create a little bit of both.

What if you decided that was a really inspiring thing to believe?

Up till now, you've either been taking charge of creating what you want or you've been busy unconsciously creating something you don't. Tell yourself the whole truth about how you landed where you are and the whole truth about whether or not you want to stay there. Remember that neither option is morally superior, and that the option you choose will simply determine the next experiences you have in your marriage.

I know you might be thinking that you need his buy-in before you can make any changes.

Maybe.

But maybe not.

What might it be like if you were willing to be wrong about needing him to be on board? What if there are actually lots of changes that you could try setting in motion right away, just because you want to?

Would you want to?

As a fun mental experiment, let's imagine the worst that could happen if you didn't wait for husband to volunteer to hold down the fort so you can go take a nap? What might happen if you didn't believe you had to stay home from girls night out because husband will be grumpy if you go? What if you even allowed yourself to try on the idea that husband's grumpiness doesn't have to be a problem?

He's a human too.

He's built to experience all of the emotions.

Just like you.

Even if he doesn't understand that truth.

Of course you can do whatever you are willing - like really and truly willing - to do to make his life comfortable. I suggest that you do. You were once in love with him after all. Might be fun to think of him that way again, in the now.

Just don't forget to do whatever you are willing to do to make YOUR life comfortable as well.

Expect that it'll feel a bit unfamiliar and maybe a little weird to prioritize your vision for your marriage and unapologetically present husband with your proposed plans.

Do it anyway.

If you want to.

Hexagon Side Six

Know that whether or not you do, you're still the same amazing and wholly valuable woman you always were.

Know that him disagreeing doesn't have to be an emergency.

Plan to use any emotions that arise as information about where to go next.

Whenever things go well, even just a little bit better than you expected, take full responsibility for creating those changes. You worked hard to make them happen. Be sure you don't skimp on the celebration. Go all in on being purposefully impressed with yourself. Because it's super fun to own your power and it's very inspiring to honor your accomplishments.

Remember, celebrating yourself doesn't take away from anyone else's work.

Even if they try to tell you it does.

All of us can - and should - celebrate our wins a lot more often. Because it's fun. And people who take responsibility for making their marriages fun are much more likely to keep creating the things they want in the relationship.

Special bonus: responsibility tends to create connection with your husband because it usually comes with high degrees of curiosity. Responsibility requires research: *What was going on here? Why did that happen? Is there another way? What's really important right now?* Responsibility asks relevant questions, even when that seems hard to do, and intentionally incorporates those answers into decisions about what to do next. Empowering questions come from love and sound like:

What's the next thing I can do to get us closer to our goal?
What do I need right now?
What do I already know how to do?
How can I connect with him best in this moment?

Disempowering questions come from fear and sound like:

Why isn't he getting it by now?
What's wrong with me?
Will we ever have more than this?
Why doesn't he care about our marriage anymore?

Remember, your brain is a problem solving machine. You are always the one who decides where your brain will focus, so why not purposefully plan to give her useful questions that assume you'll be able to figure out a satisfactory solution?

Empowering questions will help you make that happen.

Every time.

If you let it, this process of honest, judgment-free exploration could be the most engaging science experiment ever. You could decide that you're going to have a blast looking for creative new ways to claim your power in all aspects of your marriage.

The fun will flow even more freely when you remember: There's nothing wrong with you. He can't hurt your feelings. You're supposed to have all of the feelings you're experiencing and it's okay if you care what other people think. Give yourself credit for everything you did to make your marriage improve exactly as it has. Decide that continued growth in your marriage is going to be a fun process and then go make that true.

I'll be cheering for you all along the way.

How to be a Wife on Purpose

"...darling, just dive right in and follow my lead..."

- Ed Sheeran

Who doesn't love Ed Sheeran? I mean, really. He's adorably goofy looking. He's a loyal husband and a proud papa. And his voice… sigh. Everyone deserves to fall in love with Ed's rich and mellow sound in the background.

In his wildly popular song, *Perfect*, Ed invites his lady to "dive right in and follow his lead." Sounds so tempting. Who doesn't want the experience of relaxing into a loving relationship where you are completely protected, fully seen and expertly cared for?

Sign me up.

Of course you want to be with someone you can trust to lead you well.

You deserve that. And it's possible. I know this to be true.

Because that someone, the one you can trust to lead you well, is YOU.

Now, before you go on getting all disappointed and annoyed, please know that I'm not saying you'll never be able to sit back and follow your husband's lead. I'm definitely not saying that you're gonna have to do everything all by yourself in order to make your marriage work. All I'm suggesting is that maybe you choose to do yourself the favor of clearly identifying what it is that you want. Then, maybe you purposefully give yourself the gift of advocating for what you want, even if doing so feels scary or challenging.

You've just invested time and energy into reading this book. Now you have the option to decide on purpose to be the Bee you've just learned how to be.

The one who doesn't care what humans think is impossible.

The one who purposefully builds her marriage on the Hexagon Hive Stands we reviewed here together.

> Hive Stand 1 - Tell Yourself the Truth
> Hive Stand 2 - Notice your "Normal"

Conclusion

Hive Stand 3 - Dream on Purpose
Hive Stand 4 - Take Responsibility without Taking Blame
Hive Stand 5 - Celebrate the 1%
Hive Stand 6 - Don't Believe Everything you Think

How might your marriage change if you gave yourself permission to know exactly what you want in all things? And I mean permission to *really* know. Like maybe even know *out loud* kind of know.

What do you want to eat for dinner?

Where exactly do you want to place your investment resources?

How do you want him to treat you and what are you willing to accept?

Knowing the answers to those questions is the first step to making your answers your reality.

Next, ask yourself what might happen if you fully supported yourself in following your own lead about when to follow him? And supported yourself in following your own lead on when to take charge yourself? And supported yourself in following your own lead about when to chat things through a bit more before deciding anything at all?

What if you believed it was possible to do all of that self-inquiry and self-support FOR you without making any of it AGAINST him?

Sounds like freedom to me.

Marriage continuously brings you through uncharted territory.

No matter how awesome and adorable your husband is, he's not likely to be a flawless leader in every situation, all of the time. There will be times when he's flying blind. Times when he's just doing his best to figure it all out. Times when he's basically winging it. Times when he flat out flops.

Same goes for you.

You're not likely to be a flawless leader in every situation, all of the time either. There are probably times when you've actually stopped leading yourself at all. Maybe you realize you've done so. Maybe not. Either way, those times when you take your eyes off the road or your hands off the wheel are the times when things are most likely to go awry.

Voices raised.

Tears shed.

Shoulders chilled.

Hearts bruised.

All because self-leadership was relaxed too much or lost all together.

When you clue back in to how you've lost your own way, that's the perfect time to revive a close, nurturing relationship with yourself. That's the time to straighten your map and recharge your inner compass.

How great would it be to believe that you can recenter around your personal preferences and then work with him to realign your two visions, as a team, without raking one another over the coals simply because you found yourselves a bit out of sync?

What do you do when you and husband don't even agree on what being "in sync" actually means? Well… that's the exact kind of work that comes with being married.

You do the internal work of figuring out what's bothering you and why.

You do the external work of discussing all of that with him in a collaborative way.

You do the internal work of interpreting his response in as generous a way as possible.

You do the external work of supporting yourself in continued negotiations if needed.

Rinse and repeat from there.

And if at any point things go sideways, you forgive yourself and him for not handling your emotions as well as you could have. You take responsibility for anything you wish you wouldn't have done or said and you leave space for him to do the same. You do your best to stay open to making generous assumptions about his intent - and yours too.

When you can't do any of that, you say so honestly and take a break to take care of yourself in whatever way is needed to get you back into an open and collaborative headspace.

Rinse and repeat again.

One big mistake that wives tend to make in their marriages is believing that they have to be in control of everything in order to feel empowered to make a change. They focus on everything they can't control, which can get to be a pretty long list, and then feel discouraged away from exerting any sort of influence at all.

It's totally true that you can't control everything in your life or in your home.

Your husband can't either.

How fortunate that controlling EVERYTHING is not a prerequisite to useful change.

Whew.

If that was the case, we'd all be hosed.

All that's needed to start enjoying more of the marriage you thought you'd have when you said "yes!" is to actively look for places where you do have some agency - even if it's just a little bit.

Please know that I'm not inviting you to deny the truth of your experience. Not in any way. On the contrary, I want you to tell the whole truth as often as you can. Honor any pain that comes also with it. Then choose on purpose how you want to think and feel and act in the wake of whatever's gone on.

I urge you not to take this to mean you're supposed to figure out how to think happy thoughts about the crappy parts of your marriage.

That's the opposite of purpose.

Instead, tell the truth in as factual a way as possible - the less interesting the better.

He did not refill the butter dish.

The lights are still on.

He wants to spend $40 for an UBER and I do not.

He spoke to me with vocabulary and volume that I did not like.

There's a text thread in his phone that I don't much appreciate.

He didn't come to my father's funeral.

Once you've laid all the pieces of the situation out on the table, you can plan which move you want to make. You can ask yourself the following questions and really give yourself time to honestly answer:

How can I get my needs met here?

If I didn't believe (insert painful thought), what would I do next?

What is one easy-ish thing I could do, right now, to get me a little closer to my goal?

Your answers to those questions will light the way for you to continue progressing toward the marriage you really, really want to have. Make sure you answer them truthfully and often. Even if you aren't used to doing so. **Especially** if you aren't used to doing so.

If you take only one thing from the time you and I have spent together here, let it be this: Your thoughts about you and about your marriage will always be more important and more impactful than his thoughts about you or about your marriage.

Always.

Forever.

That tidbit will be true.

Because your thoughts determine the action that you will and won't take. Then the action you do or don't take determines the way your relationship plays out.

So choose your thoughts purposefully.

Tell a generous story as often as you can. About everyone you know.

Especially about you.

Because you deserve a generous story and a glorious marriage.

I know you can make that happen. Anytime you really want to. Even if it seems impossible. I know that it isn't.

Hexagon Hive Stands will help you get the exact relationship you really, really want. With yourself. With him. From here until forever.

Choose courage, now fly!

Acknowledgments

Brandon Toone
for giving me so many opportunities to be a Wife on Purpose,
for flawlessly supporting my life coaching career, for being willing to do your own thought work,
for sticking it out with me and for your sexy dancing face

Potamus, MooMees and Bear Bear
for motivating me to create an "on purpose" home for you to grow up in
I love you all beyond imagination
and I pray you'll each create your own purposeful marriages one day.

Greg and Cheryl Nyman
for hanging in, even when "happily married" was a challenge - your tenacity is inspiring

JoLynne Toone
for very possibly being the very first "Wife on Purpose" I ever witnessed

Sara Payne
for being my constant through the messy mess — no words can fully convey all you are to me
#amazonprime - #brookeandkris

Brooke Castillo
for personally demanding - to my face - that I think more of myself than I had been before

Jody Moore
for teaching me that it's okay to not want everything that's offered to me
for demonstrating that love can survive attacks made from the depths of the the tiger's cage

Bev Aron
for continuously sending me love letters - knowing full well that they may not read as such

Caryn Gillen and Melanie Fay
for cracking open my anger and holding it gently

Katie Pulsifer
for teaching me that models are just moments in time

Kara Loewentheil
for being the green screen who knows there are multiple ways to be a good feminist

Natalie Clay
for being hilarious and showing me the option to try on thoughts pretty opposite of my own
for allowing me space to not yet believe that "everything happened exactly as it should"

Brandi Downs, Brittanie Nyman, Brooke Jackson, Cheryl Nyman, Gloria Niemi, Heather Emms, Jen Jacobsen, Josie Johnson, Lu Syrett, Nikole Moon, Sara Payne
for offering your time and insight to help this manuscript shine

All of my Bees past, present and future
for sharing your vulnerable stories - it's such an honor to hold your hearts
your courage helps me help every woman who reads this book
We're changing marriages, together - #morestablehomes

Deena Rutter, Cassie Mae and Steven Novak
for making this book as pretty as possible and for taking the technical tasks off my plate

Kara Loewentheil's CCP class of August 2018
for still standing strong with each other after all this time

All the Master Coaches, Class of 2020
for all the memories made and all the breakthroughs still to come
#impeccable #illstandbyyou

Everyone Else who has believed in me or my ideas
for your open minds and willing hearts - thank you

About the Author

Candice Toone, MS is a Master Certified Life Coach and the founder of *Defying Gravity* revolution. Her mission is to help women stop wondering if they married the wrong guy and start trusting their choices again. She's a certified Deep Dive coach, Feminist coach and Faith-Based coach who hosts a group coaching program for married women who want more from their relationship. She also runs a Trauma-Informed coaching certification and teaches at The Life Coach School.

She holds a Masters degree in psychology from Utah State University and worked as a Marriage and Family Therapist before becoming a coach. She's a women's fiction author, a connoisseur of grapefruit juice and a Jazzercise enthusiast who lives in Herriman, UT with her husband, 3 children and 2 dogs.

www.candicetoone.com
https://www.facebook.com/candicetoonecoaching/
https://www.instagram.com/candicetoonecoaching/

Be a part of the Wife on Purpose movement

Join the Wife on Purpose movement and contribute your voice to the ongoing conversation by going to www.candicetoone.com and subscribing to Candice's weekly newsletter.

The *Defying Gravity* newsletter offers tips and tools to help you stop believing in what humans think is impossible and access your "inner Bee" to keep on flying anyway.

You can then dig in and do your own amazing, marriage altering work with Candice's support in her signature group coaching program, *Defying Gravity*.

Your purposeful marriage is just a few clicks away. See you on the inside.

Made in the USA
Las Vegas, NV
11 April 2022